Builders of a Nation

DR HAIFAA YOUNIS

KUBE PUBLISHING

Jannah Institute

Builders of a Nation

First published in England by

Kube Publishing Ltd,
Markfield Conference Centre,
Ratby Lane, Markfield,
Leicestershire LE67 9SY,
United Kingdom.

Distributed by

Kube Publishing Ltd.
Tel: +44(0)1530 249230
email: info@kubepublishing.com
www.kubepublishing.com

All royalty proceeds from the sale of this book go to Jannah Institute.

Cataloguing-in-Publication Data is available from the British library.

ISBN 978-1-84774-213-1 Paperback
ISBN 978-1-84774-214-8 ebook

Cover design and typesetting: Afreen Fazil (Jaryah Studios)
Printed in: Turkey

Contents

Part One: The Women of the Prophet's ﷺ Household

Part Two: Female Companions

Part Three: Female Pioneers of Islamic History

Preface

In the name of Allah, the Most Merciful, the Most Compassionate,

All praise is for Allah ﷻ, the Most Merciful, the Lord of the worlds. May peace and blessings be upon His final Prophet Muhammad ﷺ, his family and Companions, and all his followers. Allah ﷻ in His perfect wisdom and mercy bestows endless blessings upon all His servants. We experienced such an instance during an Islamic Studies course at Jannah Institute, while pondering upon *Pearls Around the Prophet ﷺ, and Muslim Women of Knowledge.*

These stories of the treasured, noble, and valuable women were not only inspirational but also practical, as they served as a blueprint for our collective future as an Ummah. This was the point of inception for *Builders of a Nation,* Ramadan 2023 series, which laid a foundation for this book. Each woman raises the other, seizing every opportunity bestowed by Allah ﷻ to reach the next level in Jannah. These women exemplify the verse in the Qur'an:

إِنَّ الْمُسْلِمِينَ وَالْمُسْلِمَاتِ وَالْمُؤْمِنِينَ وَالْمُؤْمِنَاتِ وَالْقَانِتِينَ وَالْقَانِتَاتِ وَالصَّادِقِينَ وَالصَّادِقَاتِ
وَالصَّابِرِينَ وَالصَّابِرَاتِ وَالْخَاشِعِينَ وَالْخَاشِعَاتِ وَالْمُتَصَدِّقِينَ وَالْمُتَصَدِّقَاتِ وَالصَّائِمِينَ وَالصَّائِمَاتِ
وَالْحَافِظِينَ فُرُوجَهُمْ وَالْحَافِظَاتِ وَالذَّاكِرِينَ اللَّهَ كَثِيرًا وَالذَّاكِرَاتِ أَعَدَّ اللَّهُ لَهُم مَّغْفِرَةً وَأَجْرًا عَظِيمًا

"Surely [for] Muslim men and women, believing men and women, devout men and women, truthful men and women, patient men and women, humble men and women, charitable men and women, fasting men and women, men and women who guard their chastity, and men and women who remember Allah often—for [all of] them Allah has prepared forgiveness and a great reward."

(Al-Aḥzāb 33:35)

A deliberate effort has been made in selecting these women. They are diverse, yet their roots are the same - consciousness of Allah ﷻ, unwavering obedience to Him ﷻ, and their commitment to benefit their communities with the blessings bestowed upon them.

Whether it is the vast knowledge of ʿĀ'ishah رضي الله عنها, the piety and fasting of Ḥafṣah, the warrior spirit of Nusaybah, or the pioneering medical care of Rufaydah, each woman featured in this book may serve as your role model in education, motherhood, and practicing your faith. Hence, they are deserving of the title *Builders of a Nation.*

The book is divided into three main sections. The first section centers on the wives and daughters of the Prophet Muhammad ﷺ, as the key figures in his blessed household. The second section focuses on the women around the Prophet ﷺ, the female Companions who played pivotal roles in shaping Islamic society and actively participated in the construction of a new nation, each contributing their unique qualities and characteristics. The final section showcases a selection of Muslim women throughout history, each extraordinary in their own right, harnessing distinct gifts bestowed upon them by Allah to build this Ummah.

I sincerely hope this book will remind you how far and wide the ripple effects of your good deeds will travel, enveloping and pushing forward the nation of your inheritance.

September 20th, 2023 CE/ Rabīʿ al-Awwal 5th, 1445 AH

Dr. Sh. Haifaa Younis

PART ONE

The Women of the Prophet's ﷺ Household

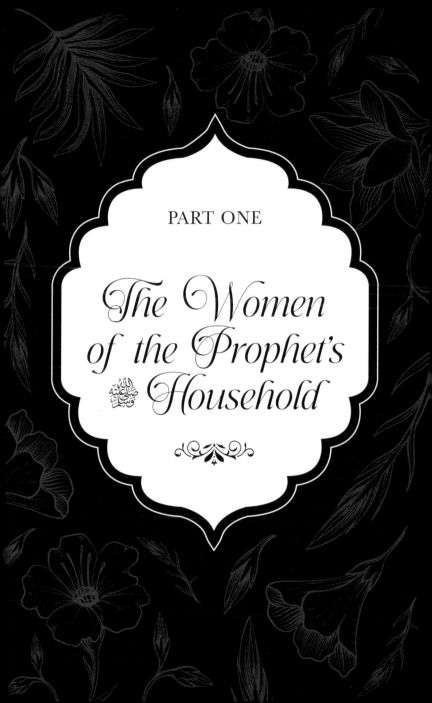

KHADĪJAH BINT KHUWAYLID رضي الله عنها

The faith of our mother Khadījah رضي الله عنها reached a height where she was given the glad tidings of a palace in Jannah by the noble angel, Jibrīl عليه السلام

CHAPTER ONE

Khadījah bint Khuwaylid ﵂

Some people are remembered long after they are gone; their names are remembered for hundreds of years after they have left this world because their contributions and achievements impact the world in such a way that history simply does not forget them. But what makes a person so memorable? What actions must we do or qualities must we possess so that thousands of years from now, people will admire and look up to us as a guiding light? There are many examples from our rich Islamic history that provide a glimpse into the lives of women who are remembered to this day. They were women who had inherent qualities and noble characters capable of building a nation with their faith, perseverance, and determination. Women who left a mark on the world and became an inspiration for all of mankind.

When analysing these inspirational women, a name that instantly comes to mind is that of Khadījah bint Khuwaylid ﵂. She was, after all, the first wife of the Prophet ﷺ and the first to accept Islam.

A Noble Beginning

Sayyidah Khadījah ﵂ was born over 1,500 years ago in the blessed city of Mecca and belonged to the clan of Banū Hāshim of the tribe of Banū Asad. When reflecting on her life, we realise that her physical appearance remains largely unknown; we do not know the colour of her eyes or the texture of her hair or how tall she was. Yet, her inner qualities – those that truly define a person – remain an example of unmatchable strength and faith till the end of time. It was these qualities that made her a builder of a nation, and by following her legacy, we too can leave our mark on this world.

Sayyidah Khadījah was born into a wealthy family. Her father was a prosperous businessman with vast wealth and industry talent. She inherited these qualities and was a successful businesswoman herself. But it was not just her wealth and success that made her famous and gave her the title of 'Princess of the Quraysh' (Amīrah Quraysh). It was her impeccable character, generous personality, and noble descent that earned her this honour. She was also called the Pure One (al-Ṭāhirah). In addition, she was well educated, literate, and was considered the most elegant woman of Mecca. These traits accompanied her throughout her life, and even though the message of Islam came to her much later, she refrained from worshipping idols. Before the Prophet ﷺ became a part of her life, she was married twice and had children, but lost both her husbands due to ravaging wars. At the young age of 25, she had already experienced the joys of motherhood and the pain of losing two husbands.

As an extremely wealthy woman of high character, it was inevitable that many respectable and noble men sought her hand in marriage. However, she declined their proposals, as her heart sought someone who possessed exceptional qualities beyond wealth and nobility.

A Blessed Union

Sayyidah Khadījah ؓ was an extremely intelligent lady who had strong business acumen. Since she did not travel with her trade caravans, she had to employ traders who would take her caravan to Yemen and Syria, which comprised the famous trade routes for the people of Mecca at the time. These traders would often return with incorrect funds, and knowing that she was being cheated, she made a desperate attempt to find an honest merchant that she could entrust with her wealth. After receiving several recommendations, Khadījah ؓ encountered the Messenger of Allah ﷺ. She entrusted him with her affairs, and as he fulfilled his duties diligently and honourably, she began to see rare attributes in him. The Prophet ﷺ had exhibited exceptional business skills, and despite his modest financial status, she recognised in him a man worthy of her admiration and love. She decided that she wanted to marry him and sent her cousin, Nafīsah, to the Prophet ﷺ to enquire if he was interested in marriage.

Upon asking about marriage, the Prophet ﷺ told Nafīsah that his modest financial situation had so far prevented him from seeking any union. Despite this, Nafīsah proceeded to suggest Khadījah ؓ for marriage. Although Khadījah ؓ was above 40 at the time and the Prophet ﷺ was 25, the only obstacle that presented concern for the Prophet ﷺ in this proposal was his poorer financial condition. The Prophet ﷺ was astonished that Khadījah ؓ would want to marry him given her nobility, wealth, beauty, and good character. Despite many obstacles, he accepted and they married.

A Pillar of Support

After accepting Islam, the faith of our mother Khadījah ﷠ reached a height where she was given the glad tidings of a palace in Jannah by the noble angel, Jibrīl ﷠.

The Prophet ﷺ said that Jibrīl ﷠ declared:

'Here is Khadījah coming to you with a dish of food or a tumbler containing something to drink. Convey to her a greeting from her Lord (Allah) and give her the glad tidings that she will have a palace in Paradise built of qaṣab (pearls and precious gems) wherein there will be neither any noise nor any fatigue (trouble).'

(al-Bukhārī)

The Prophet ﷺ also said:

'The best of the world's women is Maryam (at her lifetime), and the best of the world's women is Khadījah (at her lifetime).'

(al-Bukhārī)

What was it that made Khadījah ﷠ so beloved to Allah? When learning about the character and qualities of Khadījah ﷠, we see that the unwavering support and strength she displayed to the Prophet ﷺ when he returned from his first encounter with Jibrīl ﷠ is unmatched. Having returned from the Cave of Ḥirā', the Prophet ﷺ was shaking and repeatedly said, 'Cover me, cover me.' What had happened in the Cave of Ḥirā' was nothing ordinary. He explained to her that an angel, namely Jibrīl ﷠, had come to him, with the latter saying, 'Read.' When he responded by saying, 'I cannot read', the angel repeated his command.

He then squeezed him tightly, let him go, and said again:

اقْرَأْ بِاسْمِ رَبِّكَ الَّذِي خَلَقَ

'Read [O Prophet], in the Name of your Lord Who created.'

(al-'Alaq, 96:1)

The response of Sayyidah Khadījah and her calm and absolute faith in the Prophet ﷺ was so profound that this single event explains her superior position in his life. She was a pillar of support to him even though he was unsure about his own safety. She reassured him, reminded him of his goodness and kindness, and said words of comfort to soothe his anxious heart. In those moments of confusion, she said the following famous words to him, 'By Allah, Allah will never disgrace you, for by Allah, you maintain good relations with your kith and kin, speak the truth, help the poor and the destitute, entertain your guests generously, and assist those who are stricken with calamities.'

When he needed her the most, she was there for him with all her heart, faith, and strength. At that moment, she was not just his wife, but also a friend and somebody he could lean on – which are valuable qualities needed to build a nation.

Khadījah did not just support the Prophet ﷺ through her speech, but she also took practical steps to help him understand what had happened. Immediately, she took him to her cousin, Waraqah ibn Nawfal. Although not a Muslim, Waraqah was a monotheist and knew the past scriptures well. He said, 'What you are telling me and who came to you is the same one who came to Mūsā. If I live to the day that your people will make you leave, I will support you.' The Prophet ﷺ was shocked by this. He could not believe that his own people would push him out, but Waraqah informed him that 'no one brought to his nation what you are bringing except that they will push him to leave'.

As she stood by the side of the Prophet ﷺ, her unwavering support became the foundation upon which the message of Islam would flourish.

Belief, Devotion and Resilience

Another major reason why Khadījah is one of the leaders of Jannah is her honourable status as the first person to accept Islam. However, every honour comes with its own set of responsibilities and sacrifices, and her journey was not without its trials. She endured periods of famine, uprooting herself and her family to migrate in the face of adversity. She faced immense challenges and sacrifices, all for the sake of supporting the Prophet ﷺ and the cause they believed in. Despite her experiencing the loss of two of her own sons, she remained steadfast in her faith and found solace in the unwavering support of her four daughters.

Belief, devotion, and resilience became the pillars of Khadījah's life. She understood that success and greatness require dedication and the willingness to make sacrifices. Her noble spirit and unwavering conviction in the message of Islam made her a cornerstone in the building of a nation.

The routine of the household of the Prophet ﷺ was an example of marital bliss. Khadījah and the Prophet ﷺ would perform two units of prayer (sing. rakʿah) every morning, filling their home with the blessings of ṣalāh (prayer) even before the latter had became obligatory. She had the honour of being the mother of one of the best women in Jannah, namely Fāṭimah bint Muhammad, and the grandmother of the two masters of all the martyrs in Jannah, Sayyidunā al-Ḥasan and Sayyidunā al-Ḥusayn.

A Legacy Left Behind

The legacy that Khadījah left behind endured brilliantly with the Prophet ﷺ throughout his life. She died in Ramadan, only three days after the death of the uncle of the Prophet ﷺ, Abū Ṭālib. Her death was a result of the famine and difficulties she went through during the oppressive boycott period. The Prophet ﷺ supervised the preparation of Khadījah's grave and personally laid her down in her resting place.

Even after her passing, her memory remained etched deeply in his heart. Whenever her name was mentioned, his countenance would change, reflecting the depth of his love and admiration for her. Years after her death, when her sister Hālah would visit him in Medina, he would be overwhelmed by her memories. ʿĀ'ishah, the beloved wife of the Messenger of Allah ﷺ, recalled this poignant moment. As Hālah approached the door, the Messenger of Allah ﷺ hoped that it was Khadījah's sister who had come. His eyes filled with tears as he realised it was indeed her sister.

This is true love, and it embodies the kind of love that is rare to find. Sayyidah ʿĀ'ishah, herself a beloved woman to the Messenger of Allah ﷺ and his wife, confessed that her only source of jealousy was Khadījah – a woman she had never met.

'Ā'ishah narrated:

'I did not feel jealous of any of the wives of the Prophet ﷺ as much as I did of Khadījah despite not seeing her, but the Prophet ﷺ used to mention her very often; whenever he slaughtered a sheep, he would cut its parts and send them to the female friends of Khadījah. When I sometimes said to him, "(You treat Khadījah in such a way) as if there is no woman on Earth except Khadījah," he would say, "Khadījah was such-and-such, and from her I had children."'

(al-Bukhārī)

This was a woman who was the first among the forerunners in good deeds (al-sābiqūn al-awwalūn), the first to accept the message of Islam, the first to believe in the Messenger of Allah ﷺ, the first to give him her wholehearted support, and the first to stand firm for the truth. She was a woman whose exceptional character and selflessness shaped the destiny of a nation. Her love, her sacrifices, and her unyielding belief in the Messenger of Allah ﷺ were instrumental in the propagation of Islam. She serves as a timeless example and a symbol of strength, resilience, and devotion. Let us each search within ourselves and discover the essence of Khadījah, utilising our own unique qualities for the sake of Allah ﷻ. By doing so, we can strive to walk on her path and find a way to become builders of a nation, leaving behind a legacy of our own.

CHAPTER TWO

Sawdah bint Zamʿah ﵂

There were two types of people that played a fundamental role in the dissemination of Islam at the time of the Prophet ﷺ: 1) those who were at the forefront, who fought battles alongside him to establish the truth, and endured extreme hardships in the path of Islam, and 2) those who stayed in the background, transforming lives with their subtle presence yet strong character, and who became pillars of support, sources of comfort, and a means of strength to continue striving in the path of Allah. Sawdah bint Zamʿah ﵂ fell into the second category. Her role in the history of Islam cannot be overlooked, for her participation in the household of the Prophet ﷺ was inspirational.

A Dream Come True

Sayyidah Sawdah bint Zamʿah ﵂ was the second wife of our beloved Prophet ﷺ. She was also amongst one of the first women to accept Islam. Even though she was very different from Khadījah ﵂ in terms of a number of characteristics and traits, she possessed distinctive qualities that were essential for anyone aspiring to build a nation.

Sayyidah Sawdah ﵂ belonged to the noble tribe of Quraysh in Mecca, and was blessed with having a powerful family in both Mecca and Medina. Before her marriage to the Prophet ﷺ, she was married and had a child. When her husband died, she was left as a widow with the responsibility of being a single mother. A number of reports state that prior to the death of her first husband, both she and her husband dreamt that she would marry the Messenger of Allah ﷺ. Unable to fathom this possibility, events slowly unfolded that would turn their dreams into reality.

The Prophet ﷺ was in a state of turmoil after the death of the two people closest to him, his wife Khadījah ﵂ and his uncle Abū Ṭālib. His troubles were further compounded after the painful rejection he received from the city of Ṭā'if, where he was violently rejected. People around him saw how sad he was and how much he missed Khadījah ﵂ and suggested that he get married for his sake and for the sake of his four daughters. His concern was that due to him being a father of four daughters, it would be difficult to find someone who would want to marry him. Thus, when the name of Sawdah ﵂ came up, he delightfully agreed. She needed security, companionship, and a safe home while he needed someone affectionate to be a loving mother to his children.

Beyond Physical Beauty

Historical accounts give limited information about this remarkable woman, as she chose to live a life of obscurity even after the Prophet ﷺ. However, we do know that she possessed qualities that made her unique and a favourite among the people around her. As the wife of the Prophet ﷺ she knew her responsibility was great and honourably fulfilled her duties, taking incredible care of his daughters. She migrated twice, first to Abyssinia and then to Medina before the arrival of the Prophet ﷺ. The daughter of the Prophet ﷺ, Sayyidah Ruqayyah ﵁, who was married, migrated with her to Abyssinia. Sayyidah Sawdah's commitment and support were instrumental in nurturing a strong family unit and her unique qualities of contentment and affection helped bring a sense of peace to the life of the Prophet ﷺ.

A Heart Content with Allah ﷻ

Sayyidah Sawdah ﵁ was also a very content person, staying positive and happy with what Allah gave her; her unique optimism is something that is absolutely essential in building a nation. Striving to be content with our respective situations and taking into account all the blessings we possess is a skill we all need to adopt in our lives.

Over the years, the Prophet ﷺ married other wives for various reasons, and this is where we see how Sawdah's character truly shined. She never compared herself to anyone else, whether it was Sayyidah ʿĀ'ishah, Sayyidah Zaynab, or Sayyidah Umm Salamah ﵁. Rather than dwelling on what she thought she might lack in comparison to others, she focused on utilising her unique attributes to leave a lasting legacy. Her character reminds us of a beautiful narration where the Prophet ﷺ said:

'Wealth is not found in having many possessions, but rather (true) wealth is feeling sufficiency in the soul.'

(al-Bukhārī)

It was Sayyidah Sawdah's beautiful quality of contentment that also made her a favourite among the wives of the Prophet ﷺ. This was to the extent that 'Ā'ishah ؓ said that she never wished to be another woman save one figure: Sayyidah Sawdah ؓ. Sayyidah Sawdah was devoted to her worship. She wanted to spend more time in worshipping Allah and even ended up selflessly allotting her day to Sayyidah 'Ā'ishah ؓ. She had a generous spirit and admirable dedication to charity (ṣadaqah). Assuming the role of a motherly figure in the nascent Muslim society, she was always looking out for those in need.

Joy in the Home of the Prophet ﷺ

Amidst her devoutness, she also had a delightful sense of humour. On one occasion, during a prolonged prostration in prayer led by the Prophet ﷺ, she humorously remarked that the prostration was so lengthy that she felt her nose might bleed.

Another humorous incident that left the Prophet ﷺ smiling was the following. During a conversation among the Prophet's wives ؓ about the False Messiah (Dajjāl), Sayyidah Sawdah ؓ became frightened and started running. She was frightened that he was about to come. When the Prophet ﷺ brought her back and reassured her that his appearance was not going to occur in their time, she looked down and started laughing.

This was the character of Sayyidah Sawdah ؓ. The woman who filled the home of the Prophet ﷺ with laughter and joy. The woman who became his source of comfort at his time of extreme sadness and helped him give a loving home to his daughters.

Sayyidah Sawdah lived her life after the death of the Prophet ﷺ in peace with everyone around her. She died in Medina and was buried in the sacred city's graveyard, which is known as al-Baqīʿ. Without a single complaint or ill-feeling, she was remembered for her generosity and selflessness – the attributes needed to build a home, to build a nation, and to bring change to society.

‘Ā’ISHAH BINT ABĪ BAKR ﵂

Her vast knowledge and impeccable memory were her greatest contributions to the Muslim ummah, with many of the rulings that we know today coming as a result of her inquisitive nature.

CHAPTER THREE

ʿĀ'ishah bint Abī Bakr ﵂

We often hear stories of people who lived impressionable lives and had qualities that made them rise above others. But few come close to this legendary woman, whose unique attributes and impressive personality made her a cherished figure in the history of the Muslim world. This is the story of a woman whose life was woven with beauty, challenges, and invaluable lessons for us all. This is the story of Sayyidah ʿĀ'ishah ﵂, the daughter of Abū Bakr ﵁ and Sayyidah Umm Rūmān ﵂ and the wife and most beloved person to our Prophet Muhammad ﷺ.

An Example of Beauty and Brilliance

Sayyidah ʿĀ'ishah ﵂ belonged to the Quraysh tribe of Mecca. She was born approximately four years prior to the prophethood of the Messenger ﷺ and grew up in a Muslim house. Her father, Abū Bakr ﵁, was a dear friend and Companion of the Prophet ﷺ. Sayyidah ʿĀ'ishah ﵂ was her father's favourite, since she was endowed with qualities that set her apart from others even as a child. Historical records give a fairly elaborate description of her uniqueness, describing at least ten characteristics about her that each one of us would love to possess.

Sayyidah 'Ā'ishah ﷢ was blessed with beauty and grace, and was further complemented by a delicate figure. Her aspirations soared beyond this world, and her ambitious nature was focused on divinity and eternal reward. She was extremely observant and was known for her intelligence, articulation, and impeccable memory. Although she grew up in the household of the Prophet ﷺ, her knowledge reached beyond matters of religion. She did not just excel in Islamic jurisprudence but also had deep knowledge of poetry, dentistry, and medicine, with the latter being one of her landmarks. Curious about the depths of her knowledge, she was questioned about her medical know-how. To this, she explained that when the tribes and Bedouins came to the Prophet ﷺ and presented their ailments, he would teach them about prophetic medicine. Her observant nature and sharp memory allowed her to learn and retain all the information, and she eventually gained a vast level of understanding in this field. These skills also lent to her ability to narrate thousands of Hadiths that continue to benefit us today.

Her vast knowledge and impeccable memory were her greatest contributions to the Muslim ummah, with many of the rulings that we know today coming as a result of her inquisitive nature. The ruling of tayammum (dry ablution), which is the permissibility of using dust to make wuḍū' when water is not available, only arose due to the famous incident of the lost necklace. At first, it seemed quite unfortunate for everyone to be searching for 'Ā'ishah's lost necklace in a remote and barren plane without any water for their religious needs, but it served as an eventual blessing when the verse of tayammum was revealed.

Perhaps one of Sayyidah ʿĀ'ishah's main favours upon the Muslim ummah was her habit of asking questions. She was quite inquisitive by nature and this contributed to the vast knowledge she gathered and imparted among the future generations. She was not shy to ask about things that most people shied away from. One such example is when she noted to the Prophet ﷺ that the men obtain the best reward – they go for fighting and we do not, she added, but we want that reward in the afterlife too. To this he ﷺ responded:

لَٰكِنَّ أَفْضَلَ الْجِهَادِ حَجٌّ مَبْرُورٌ

'You have the best act of jihad without going out for fighting, and that is Hajj Mabrūr (i.e. a pilgrimage that is done excellently with no faults).

(al-Bukhārī)

She also asked the Prophet ﷺ to assign a nickname (kunyah) to her as he had assigned to all his other wives. She asked him, 'I want you to give me a nickname. What is the nickname you want to give me?' In response, he called her the Mother of ʿAbdullāh (Umm ʿAbdullāh); even though she did not have children, her praiseworthy attributes and status in Islam gave her the honour of becoming the mother of all believers – a source of motivation and comfort for us all. We learn from Sayyidah ʿĀ'ishah ؓ that when Allah ﷻ takes an obvious blessing from us or keeps us from something that our heart yearns so fervently for, we need to have strong faith that He will give us something much better in its place. This is just as Allah ﷻ gifted ʿĀ'ishah ؓ with the immense love of the Prophet ﷺ, wisdom and knowledge, and an unmatched status among the Muslims.

A Selfless, Joyful Heart

Sayyidah ʿĀʾishah ☙ possessed a distinctive charitable and considerate nature. She would give in charity everything that came her way without keeping any of it for herself. Her desire to please Allah ﷻ was far greater than love for the material of this world, and this is evident from a famous story that shines light on her selflessness and compassion. She was known to fast frequently and on an occasion when she was fasting, Sayyidunā ʿUmar ☙, who was the Caliph at the time, sent her an allowance for the month. Without a pause, Sayyidah ʿĀʾishah ☙ ordered her helper to distribute all of it among the needy people. When the time for breaking her fast came and she enquired about the food, her helper reminded her that all the money was distributed and that there was nothing to buy food with. Her helper asked her why she did not keep some of it so that they could buy something, but she simply replied that it had not crossed her mind to do such a thing. This is a clear example of how her selflessness and empathy for others outweighed her own needs.

Sayyidah ʿĀʾishah ☙ also had a humorous side and often joked with the Prophet ﷺ, bringing laughter and happiness to his life. It is reported that she once said to him that there is a horse that has two wings. In amazement, the Prophet ﷺ asked how that was possible, to which she replied that Sulaymān ☙ had a horse with two wings. The Messenger of Allah ﷺ laughed and agreed that she was indeed right. In this story, we see just a glimpse of the beautiful bond they shared, with respect, love, and compassion at its core.

ʿĀ'ishah ﵄ also had a playful side to her and often shared joyful moments of laughter and fun with the Prophet ﷺ. A famous example of this is when she raced with him and won. In a similar race much later, the Prophet ﷺ was able to beat her. He laughed and light-heartedly told her that this victory settles the score for the race he lost!

A Match Made in Heaven

It is said that matches are made in heaven, and this is true in the sense that Allah ﷻ is the One Who chooses our life partners for us, but for Sayyidah ʿĀ'ishah ﵄ and our beloved Prophet ﷺ this was a literal reality. Their marriage was finalised by Allah ﷻ and Sayyidah ʿĀ'ishah ﵄ was shown to the Prophet ﷺ twice in his dreams. He described that in one of the dreams, he saw a picture on a piece of silk and when he lifted it to see the picture, it was hers. In another dream, he saw that he visited Abū Bakr ﵁, asking for her hand.

They were companions in good and bad, happiness and grief, and most of all, in faith. She supported him in every way, being there by his side through the tough times and joining hands in his triumphs. Her presence in his life filled the void that the absence of Sayyidah Khadījah ﵄ had created. She was his beloved, one whose companionship he cherished the most. His love for her was so profound that when one of the Companions, namely ʿAmr ibn al-ʿĀṣ ﵁, asked him who his most beloved person was, he said that it was ʿĀ'ishah ﵄. He was asked next about his beloved person from amongst the men, and he said, 'Her father.' While Sayyidunā ʿAmr ibn al-ʿĀṣ ﵁ was hoping to hear his name, the Prophet ﷺ

even mentioned Abū Bakr with reference to his beloved wife, ʿĀ'ishah. How special she was to him that everything associated with her became unique and priceless for him.

They found comfort in each other's presence. Their simple and humble lifestyle did not keep them from enjoying each other's company. We get a glimpse of this affection from one of their personal moments shared with us, where one night he ﷺ was standing up in ṣalāh. As their room was quite small, her feet came close to his feet while he was standing. When he finished, the Prophet ﷺ asked her to leave him with his Lord, that is, with Allah ﷻ. She just looked at him and said that she loves him and wants to be close to him. This was their compassion and affection for each other.

They could read each other's feelings and emotions even without words. The Prophet ﷺ once said to ʿĀ'ishah, 'I know when you are happy with me and I know when you are upset with me.' She said, 'How is that?' And he said, 'When you are happy with me, you say, "By the Lord of Muhammad." And if you are not happy with me, you say, "By the Lord of Ibrāhīm."' And she said, 'By Allah, it is only my tongue which does not say your name, but your name is in my heart. And my heart will never let you go.'

An Unending Quest for Improvement

Sayyidah ʿĀ'ishah yearned for perfection in everything she did. She would often ask the Prophet ﷺ questions on how she could improve her character and disposition (akhlāq). On one occasion, she had a gift that she wanted to give to one of her two neighbours. One was to the left and the other to the right. She was confused about which of them to give it to and so she asked the Prophet ﷺ for advice. His advice was – and this is something that we all learn from this narration – that we should first choose the door that is closest to ours.

We have so much to be thankful to her, for her questions and concerns gave us pearls of wisdom that will forever fill our lives with radiance. She is the leading female narrator of Hadiths, having related 2,210 Hadiths from the Prophet ﷺ, bringing her fifth among all the narrators, with Sayyidunā Abū Hurayrah ؓ at the top.

A Test of Resilience

It is the sunnah of this life that blessings often come hand in hand with trials and tribulations. The more blessed a person is, the more Allah ﷻ tests their resilience and strength of faith. Sayyidah ʿĀ'ishah ؓ, the most beloved to the Prophet ﷺ, the daughter of the esteemed Abū Bakr ؓ, and a woman of remarkable beauty, intelligence, and knowledge, was no exception to this rule. In fact, her test was harder than most due to her high status in Islam.

Her test, just as her attributes, was unique. She narrated the painful incident years later, showing us that she was an embodiment of resilience and strength of faith. The context of the story is that whenever the Prophet ﷺ would go on an expedition, he would take one or more of his wives along the journey. In this particular incident, Sayyidah ʿĀ'ishah ؓ accompanied him on his trip. On their way back, she needed to go and relieve herself, and since they did not have the facilities that we have in the modern age, they would have to find a secluded place which was usually far from the camp. On her way back, she noticed that her necklace, which was a gift from her sister Asmā' ﷺ and was very dear to her, was lost. She began looking for this necklace, and by the time she found it and came back, the caravan had gone.

It may seem strange that the caravan left such an important person behind, but when we read the historical records, we find that her petite build and light weight made it difficult for them to feel any difference. When they got up to leave, they assumed that she was safely sitting atop the camel. Hence, they left, not knowing that Sayyidah 'Ā'ishah ﷺ was left alone in the desert. This is where we see her courage and strength, as she did not lose her calm. Undeterred, she steeled herself for what lay ahead, knowing that the Prophet ﷺ had appointed a companion to trail behind the caravan. This was a habit of the Prophet ﷺ in case someone was left behind or something was lost.

Her prayers were answered when Ṣafwān ﷺ, a Companion, came about with his camel to make sure nothing was left behind. This was the time before the verses of hijab were revealed whereby the faces of the Prophet's wives were ordered to be completely covered, so he was able to identify her. Her description of the incident depicts a clear picture of how both these honourable souls displayed remarkable modesty and wisdom. With a mere cough, Ṣafwān allowed her to mount his camel, avoiding any unnecessary gaze. His honourable conduct and her unwavering trust in Allah ﷻ guided her through this unexpected ordeal. As they entered Medina, whispers began to circulate about the encounter between Sayyidah 'Ā'ishah ﷺ and Ṣafwān ﷺ. 'Abdullāh ibn Ubayy, the leader of the hypocrites, seized this opportunity to sow seeds of doubt and rumours. His false insinuations and slander soon spread like wildfire through the town, challenging the integrity of Sayyidah 'Ā'ishah ؓ and testing the faith of the believers.

She narrated those painful days in her own words, saying, 'When I arrived, I became ill. I was not feeling well. I only noticed that the Prophet ﷺ was not treating me the same way. Usually, when I am sick, he asks me about me. This time he is asking about me, but it is not the same way. He is different.' She had the same feeling that every wife has when her husband seems different, but she shrugged it off thinking that maybe there was something else on his mind. Consequently, she asked him, 'Can I go and stay with my mother and father until I feel better?' And he gave her permission to go.

Looking for Answers

Meanwhile, there was no revelation of the Qur'an in Medina. The gossip and abominable rumours were the talk of the town and the Prophet ﷺ was in deep grief. Without any revelation and guidance from above, the Prophet ﷺ sought to ask her servant about her, as was communicated by Allah ﷻ. She said, 'I do not know anything but all good (khayr). The only fault she has is if I have prepared the dough and I tell her to keep an eye on it, she will go and play and leave the dough and then the sheep will come and eat it. Otherwise, this woman has no faults.' He also consulted Sayyidunā 'Alī ؓ, who said, 'O Prophet, we do not know anything but good about her.'

In the same duration, while she was still at her parent's house, she went out one day to relieve herself. A relative of hers and her father's, the mother of a Companion named Misṭaḥ, accompanied her. As she was helping her, Sayyidah ʿĀ'ishah ؓ tripped, but did not fall. At this, her relative said out loud, 'Woe upon Misṭaḥ!' Sayyidah ʿĀ'ishah ؓ was shocked and said, 'Why are you saying this? This is a man who attended Badr. This is a Companion, and this is a very righteous man.' She said, 'You do not know what he said about you.' And when she told her the horrible things that people were saying and the rumours going around, Sayyidah ʿĀ'ishah ؓ was struck with grief. She could not believe that people were slandering her and saying this about her, especially the Prophet ﷺ. She asked her in disbelief, 'Does the Prophet ﷺ know?' And the woman said, 'Yes.' Sayyidah ʿĀ'ishah ؓ said that for the next three days, she did not stop crying for a moment. Her heart was filled with such sorrow that she felt as if it would burst open with pain. Yet, Sayyidah ʿĀ'ishah ؓ remained steadfast in her faith and resilience. The cruel accusations did not break her spirit, nor did they shake her faith in Allah's plan. She knew that her reputation and innocence rested in Allah's Hand, and she entrusted her fate to Him alone.

She continued to stay at the house of her parents. The Prophet ﷺ visited her one day and sat across from her as she cried. He said, 'O ʿĀ'ishah, if what they are saying is true, say it and ask Allah ﷻ for forgiveness, and He will forgive you.' She said that the moment he said this, her tears stopped. Her eyes went dry as she could not believe her ears. She only looked towards her father and asked him to respond to this accusation. He remained silent. She looked towards her mother, hoping to hear words that would defend her and announce her innocence. There were none. The silence around them was palpable, and with a sinking feeling, she pronounced,'I am not going to say anything but what the father of Yūsuf ؑ said,' and then she commented, 'He said to his sons, "beautiful patience" and I have turned my back to everybody.'

The Triumph of Faith

What strong faith she had! Her conviction in Allah's plan is a lesson for us to firmly believe that He will never leave us alone. She knew Allah ﷻ would bring the truth in front of everyone and that is exactly what happened. The moment she handed her affairs over to Allah, she felt something change in the Prophet ﷺ. Allah ﷻ, in His infinite wisdom, revealed verses of Sūrah al-Nūr, clearing Sayyidah 'Ā'ishah ؓ of any wrongdoing. Her innocence was proclaimed, and those who propagated lies were chastised.

إِنَّ الَّذِينَ جَاءُوا بِالْإِفْكِ عُصْبَةٌ مِّنكُمْ ۚ لَا تَحْسَبُوهُ شَرًّا لَّكُم بَلْ هُوَ خَيْرٌ لَّكُمْ

'Indeed, those who came up with that slander are a group of you. Do not think this is bad for you. Rather, it is good for you.'

(al-Nūr, 24:11)

He looked at her and said, 'O 'Ā'ishah, your innocence came.' It was a moment to rejoice for both Abū Bakr ؓ and her mother. He embraced her and asked her to hug the Prophet ﷺ and thank him. However, she said, 'No, I am not going to give thanks except to the One Who knew I was innocent and Who sent my innocence – Allah ﷻ.' And then she said, 'I knew I was innocent and I knew

Allah ﷻ would show my innocence, but I never thought that I was so worthy in the sight of Allah ﷻ that entire verses of the Qur'an would be revealed proclaiming my innocence and that they will be read until the end of days.'

Honoured and Revered

The trial that Sayyidah 'Ā'ishah went through was unimaginable, but so was the honour she received from being defended by Allah ﷻ. It was unlike anything she expected, and the words of Allah ﷻ comforted her and took away all the pain. 'Ā'ishah's honour was also exemplified in her being the closest in proximity to the Prophet ﷺ at the time of his death. He died on her chest and just moments before his death, he desired to use the miswāk (cleaning twig made from the Salvadora tree). She said, 'I noticed someone using a miswāk and I felt that the Prophet ﷺ wanted it, so I took it from the Companion, moistened it with my saliva, and put it in his mouth.' And then she said, 'The last thing he tasted was my saliva.'

He passed away in her house and in her embrace. She was by his side till the end, comforting him and supplicating for him. She lived many years after him and continued sharing her immense wisdom and knowledge with the Companions. Sayyidah 'Ā'ishah was the most knowledgeable woman in Medina, with prominent Companions taking her opinion and advice about rulings and Islamic jurisprudence. Her insight and understanding of matters of the religion gave her a command that few had.

She passed away on the 17th of Ramadan at the age of 66, leaving behind a legacy till the end of time. Her courage, intelligence, and unwavering faith in Allah ﷻ are a testament to the resilience and strength that our faith bestows upon us as Muslims. As we continue to honour and cherish her legacy, may we draw inspiration from her unwavering devotion to Allah ﷻ, her ability to endure, and her unyielding faith in the face of adversity.

ḤAFṢAH BINT ʿUMAR ﵄

She was described as a person who was frequently fasting and constantly in observance of the night prayer. This was to the point that even in her final moments, she was fasting, a reflection of her deep connection with Allah ﷻ.

CHAPTER FOUR

Ḥafṣah bint ʿUmar ﷦

*I*t is human nature to feel pride in our lineage, our ancestry, and the family we belong to. Being connected to people with influence is something we all yearn for. Imagine if you could claim to be close to the best human created by Allah ﷻ, that is, His Messenger ﷺ. And not just being close to him, but becoming a part of his life as his companion and wife. That is a place of honour and blessing. A place worth more than anything else in the world. This was the place that Allah ﷻ gifted to Sayyidah Ḥafṣah ﷦, the daughter of Sayyidunā ʿUmar ﷦, who was not just a Companion of the Prophet ﷺ but also his dear friend.

An Unexpected Companionship

Sayyidah Ḥafṣah ﷦ grew up in Mecca and belonged to a noble family. She preceded her father in accepting the message of Islam and was a firm believer. Before her marriage with the Prophet ﷺ, she was married to a Companion named Khunays ﷦, who was martyred in the Battle of Badr, leaving her a widow at the tender age of 21.

Sayyidunā ʿUmar ﷦ had accepted Islam at this point, and worried about his daughter's future. He wished to marry her with someone of high integrity and character, and with this intention, he approached Sayyidunā ʿUthmān ؓ. When he did not receive a response from Sayyidunā ʿUthmān ؓ, he approached Sayyidunā ʿAlī ؓ, who also remained silent. This made Sayyidunā ʿUmar ؓ extremely upset, and he went to the Prophet ﷺ to express his disappointment about the fact that two of his closest friends and companions did not want to marry his daughter.

The Prophet ﷺ in his supreme wisdom knew how to console ʿUmar and make him feel better. He said, 'Ḥafṣah will marry better than ʿUthmān and ʿAlī. And ʿUthmān will marry better than Ḥafṣah.' This proved to be true, as indeed, Ḥafṣah ؓ was married to the Prophet ﷺ, who was the best of mankind and better than both ʿUthmān and ʿAlī ؓ, while Sayyidunā ʿUthmān ؓ was married to the daughter of the Prophet ﷺ, Sayyidah Umm Kulthūm ؓ, who was better than Ḥafṣah ؓ.

Exceptional Worship and Trust

Sayyidah Ḥafṣah ؓ had numerous unique qualities, and one of them was her exceptional worship. She would stand in ṣalāh for hours and was known for her acts of devotion, such as spending long spans of time pondering over the Qur'an. She was an excellent writer and was proficient in reading and writing, thereby adopting her father's sharpness and intelligence. With these attributes, it is not a surprise that she memorised the entire Qur'an, being one of the few female Companions to have achieved such an undertaking. The beauty of her character included a special element, which was trustworthiness. It was this quality of being trustworthy that made Sayyidunā Abū Bakr ؓ entrust the only copy of the Qur'an with her. This remained the case until

Sayyidunā ʿUthmān ؓ decided to make more copies of it and send them to other countries. When he requested the copy kept with her, she happily obliged. This was the copy through which all the others were written by the 'writers of revelation'.

Navigating Emotions and Jealousy

It is inevitable that when women live together and are required to distribute their time with their husband, there will be an element of jealousy and frustration between them. It was well known that Sayyidah ʿĀ'ishah ؓ held a special place in the heart of the Prophet ﷺ, a fact that sometimes stirred feelings of jealousy in Sayyidah Ḥafṣah ؓ. Consequently, in order to put her anxious feelings to rest, Sayyidunā ʿUmar ؓ visited his daughter and said the following to her: 'My little daughter, my beautiful daughter, do not be misled by the one whom the Prophet ﷺ has more love for.' He reassured her that she was special in her own way and comforted her. Her father's tender words reminded her of her worth and the unique bond they shared. When Sayyidunā ʿUmar ؓ shared this with the Prophet ﷺ, he smiled, demonstrating his human nature and deep understanding of the feelings of others. This example conveys to us that even though we cannot control our emotions sometimes and feel things that we do not wish to experience, we can still navigate them with guidance and wisdom.

Both Sayyidah ʿĀ'ishah and Sayyidah Ḥafṣah ؓ were special in their own right, but it was only natural that there was jealousy between them in the beginning. They were both married to the noblest man to exist, the Prophet ﷺ. A man who was the best to his family, friends, and all of mankind. But what was admirable about these two women was how their faith, noble character, and goodness of heart converted this jealousy into an enduring friendship. Their love for Allah ﷻ and His Messenger ﷺ bridged the gaps, and they became inseparable companions, with their bond strengthened by shared acts of worship and devotion.

This friendship is beautifully depicted in an interesting narration related by ʿĀʾishah ﵂, where the Prophet ﷺ entered, and he found her and Sayyidah Ḥafṣah ﵂ together. She narrated the report in the following fashion: Ḥafṣah spoke before me and she said, "O Messenger of Allah, ʿĀʾishah and I woke up with the intention of fasting. However, the food was given to us as a gift, and we broke our fast because the food was given to us as a gift.'" The Prophet ﷺ told them not to worry and that the fast could be made up later. This narration paints a beautiful picture of how they worshipped Allah ﷻ together. They forgot their differences and became partners in devotion, seeking the pleasure of Allah ﷻ and encouraging each other towards goodness. They shared a sweet bond of selfless love and friendship. A bond that only the love of Allah ﷻ and His Messenger ﷺ could create.

Sayyidah Ḥafṣah ﵂ was also witty like her father, and this was exemplified in her feelings of jealousy towards another of the Prophet's wives, Sayyidah Ṣafiyyah ﵂. Sayyidah Ṣafiyyah ﵂ was extremely beautiful and belonged to a Jewish tribe before accepting Islam, which made it hard for others to get along with her. In a particular incident, as the Prophet ﷺ entered upon Sayyidah Ṣafiyyah ﵂, he found her crying. When he asked her why she was crying, she told him the following: Ḥafṣah said to me, "You are the daughter of a Jew."' The Prophet ﷺ comforted her and said, 'Why are you crying? Say to her, "My father is a

Prophet, my uncle is a Prophet, and my husband is a Prophet, so why do you think you are better than me?"' He was referring to Prophet Mūsā 🌸, Prophet Hārūn 🌸, and himself 🌸. He also reprimanded Sayyidah Ḥafṣah 🌸 for this and said, 'O Ḥafṣah, be fearful of Allah.' He was truly remarkable in the way he was able to make peace between hearts that had differences. He knew how to maintain balance between them and give each of them their rights.

Yet again, we see that no matter what these women felt for each other in the beginning, the love of Allah 🌸 and His Messenger 🌸 always dissolved their differences and brought them together. The distinguishing quality of these legendary women was that the fear of Allah 🌸 was enough to put them off of anything undesirable.

Inspiring Revelation

Sayyidah Ḥafṣah 🌸 was also another of the wives of the Prophet 🌸 concerning whom verses of the Qur'an were revealed. These were the first four verses of Sūrah al-Taḥrīm, which is the 66th chapter of the Qur'an. One of the commentaries on the sūrah describes its context, stating that Sayyidah 'Ā'ishah 🌸 and Sayyidah Ḥafṣah 🌸 had become extremely close. The Prophet 🌸 in his routine used to spend time with his wives equally in the day, staying a night at each of the wife's house. Both Sayyidah 'Ā'ishah 🌸 and Sayyidah Ḥafṣah 🌸 noticed that the Prophet 🌸 was staying a little bit longer with Sayyidah Zaynab bint Jaḥsh 🌸. As she was very beautiful, they both became jealous and made a plan. They decided that the next time he came from the house of Sayyidah Zaynab 🌸, they would tell him that there was a bad smell coming from his mouth and ask him what he ate at her house to get that smell. This way, he would become cognisant and shorten his time with Sayyidah Zaynab ؓ. Thus, when the Prophet ﷺ visited Sayyidah Ḥafṣah ؓ, she asked him about it, and the same happened when he visited Sayyidah ʿĀ'ishah ؓ. The Prophet ﷺ was perturbed by this and decided to never eat the honey that Sayyidah Zaynab ؓ lovingly served him again, as he understood this to be the cause of the strange smell.

But Allah ﷻ knew the plan and sent revelation with a clear command:

يَـٰٓأَيُّهَا ٱلنَّبِيُّ لِمَ تُحَرِّمُ مَآ أَحَلَّ ٱللَّهُ لَكَ تَبْتَغِي مَرْضَاتَ أَزْوَٰجِكَ وَٱللَّهُ غَفُورٌ رَّحِيمٌ

'O Prophet! Why do you prohibit from what Allah has made lawful to you, seeking to please your wives? And Allah is All-Forgiving, Most Merciful.'

(al-Taḥrīm, 66:1)

Allah ﷻ revealed to the Prophet ﷺ that this was planned by his two wives, and He ﷻ gave them two options: either to repent and have their hearts cleansed and purified or continue on their way and get divorced from the Prophet ﷺ. This is because although their status was high, their responsibility and accountability were even higher. They were the role models of the coming generations and for all of humanity until the end of times.

Therefore, any misstep by them would affect others in a much larger magnitude than if the same act was performed by any other human being.

Testing Times and Triumph over Trials

Another unique incident that happened in the life of Sayyidah Ḥafṣah ؓ was that the Prophet ﷺ either planned to divorce Sayyidah Ḥafṣah ؓ or had divorced her. We find mention of this in the books of sīrah, tafsīr, and other commentary works. We do not find details about the reason for this, except that the marriage was reconciled before the expiry of the ʿiddah, which is the waiting period for divorce. What a test it must have been to be the daughter of a great Companion, Sayyidunā ʿUmar ؓ and the wife of the Prophet ﷺ and find yourself at the threshold of being divorced by the greatest man to ever live. It made Sayyidunā ʿUmar ؓ distraught and he even talked to her about it to smooth out the matter.

This was a woman who went through turbulent times but emerged as one of the most pious women in the history of Islam. She was described as a person who was frequently fasting and constantly in observance of the night prayer (ṣawwāmah, qawwāmah). This was to the point that even in her final moments, she was fasting, a reflection of her deep connection with Allah ﷻ. She died at the age of 59 at the time of Muʿāwiyah ؓ and was buried in Jannah al-Baqīʿ next to the mosque of the Prophet ﷺ. Her janāzah prayer was led by the governor of Medina, Marwān ibn al-Ḥakam.

CHAPTER FIVE

Zaynab bint Khuzaymah رضي الله عنها

There is a common saying that speaks of how it is not important how long we live but how well we live. Essentially, it is our actions and dealings with others that define who we are and ultimately decide if we live on in people's memories. True to this saying, the impressive life of Zaynab bint Khuzaymah رضي الله عنها, the daughter of Khuzaymah and the fifth wife of the Prophet ﷺ, was short but truly inspirational.

Sayyidah Zaynab رضي الله عنها belonged to the Quraysh tribe of Mecca. She was a widow, as her husband ʿUbaydah ibn al-Ḥārith was martyred in the Battle of Badr. As was common custom, most widows of Badr were looking to get married, but that was not the case with Sayyidah Zaynab رضي الله عنها. She relied on Allah عز وجل alone to support her and take care of her. But Allah عز وجل had a plan for her and she was blessed with the companionship of the Messenger of Allah عز وجل. Her half-sister, Sayyidah Maymūnah رضي الله عنها, was later married to the Prophet ﷺ too, endowing their family with divine blessings.

The Mother of the Poor (Umm al-Masākīn)

Sayyidah Zaynab ؓ lived less than a year after getting married to the Prophet ﷺ, but in that short life span, she was a source of help and relief to many, earning the honourable title of 'The Mother of the Poor and Needy' (Umm al-Masākīn). She was known to be extremely compassionate, looking out for the needy, consistently tending to the needs of those less fortunate, and touching their lives with her kindness.

Her limited time on Earth teaches us a profound truth: it is not the quantity of our deeds but the consistency of our actions that matter most in the sight of Allah ﷻ. The legacy of Sayyidah Zaynab ؓ was forged through continuous acts of goodness and compassion. It teaches us that all it takes is a moment for us to change something for the better, make a difference in someone's life, and leave behind a good deed that will forever benefit us and others. This Hadith narrated by Sayyidah 'Ā'ishah ؓ shines light on this concept perfectly:

'The most beloved deeds to Allah are those done regularly, even if they are little.'

(al-Bukhārī, 6462)

However, it is essential to remember that our good deeds alone will not take us to Jannah; without the mercy of Allah ﷻ, everything is insufficient. Sayyidah Zaynab's life exemplifies the beauty of simplicity and hidden virtues. Allah ﷻ treasures those who have pure hearts and those who are conscious of Him, even if they remain unknown in this world. It is not fame or popularity but our devotion and closeness to Him that defines our worth in front of Him. Making small changes in our lives, helping those in need, even if little, picking up a good habit or a good act can, over time, take us higher on the scale of good deeds and eventually fill our lives with Allah's blessings.

A Life of Devotion

Sayyidah Zaynab ﵂ led her life in devotion, her days marked by exceptional compassion and kindness to others. This was perhaps the reason for why Allah ﷻ chose her for the Prophet ﷺ, as the qualities that defined her made her noble and praiseworthy.

Allah ﷻ loves those who have three characteristics: purity, Allah-consciousness, and invisibility (the one who is not very well known). The Messenger of Allah ﷺ said:

إن الله يحب العبد التقي الغني الخفي

'Allah loves a slave who is pious, free of all wants and the unnoticed.'

(Muslim)

Allah ﷻ also says in Sūrah al-Nisā' that there are Prophets whose names are not revealed to us but they are still Prophets in the sight of Allah ﷻ. Surayj reported that the Messenger of Allah ﷺ said:

'If Allah Almighty wills goodness for a servant, He sweetens him.' It was said, 'What is his sweetness?' The Prophet ﷺ said, 'Allah Almighty opens the door of righteous deeds for him before his death and then receives his soul in that state.'

(Musnad Aḥmad, 17784)

We have all heard of people who accept Islam and barely get the time to do any good deeds. They spend their last days striving for the pleasure of Allah ﷻ, making continuous efforts to collect as many blessings as they can. This was the case with Sayyidah Zaynab رضي الله عنها, who did not even get a year with the Prophet ﷺ but made sure to turn each moment into an act of goodness. So much so that we remember her, honour her, and learn from her example to this day. Her story reminds us that our worth lies not in worldly recognition, but in the eyes of Allah ﷻ. She was the second wife to die at the time of the Prophet ﷺ, and he prayed on her. May Allah ﷻ be pleased with her and may we all strive to leave behind a legacy of compassion and devotion, just as she did.

UMM SALAMAH رضي الله عنها

The believing, devout, truthful, patient, humble, charitable, modest, and fearful of Allah عز وجل will have equal rewards, regardless of whether they are men or women.

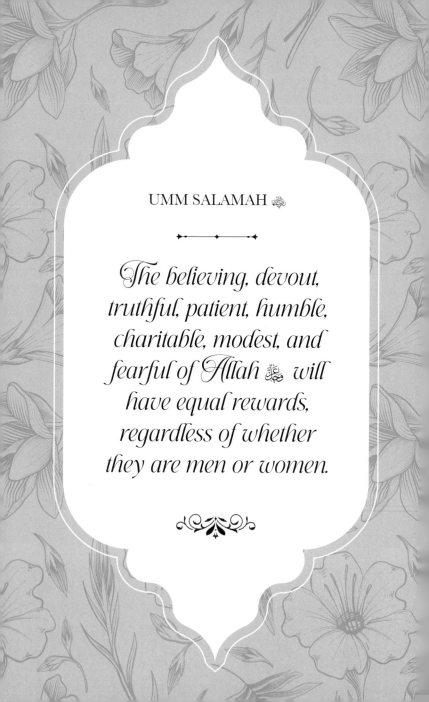

CHAPTER SIX

Umm Salamah ﵂

Getting to know the wives of the Prophet ﷺ, we find that even though they were all unique in their own ways, they shared common qualities of wisdom, faith, and inspirational character. Each of them served as a guiding light to the future generations, and left their mark on the history of the world. Their courage, resilience, and foresight were unmatched, as they were chosen for the noblest of all men, the Prophet of Allah ﷺ. When perusing these admirable characteristics, a name we associate and all know very well is Umm Salamah ﵂, one of the wives of the Prophet ﷺ, who was renowned for her exceptional wisdom and courage.

Her real name was Hind bint Abī Umayyah, but she is widely known by her nickname, Umm Salamah ﵂. Her life was filled with many paradigm-shaping incidents that made her an integral builder of the Islamic nation.

Heartbreak and a Miracle

The story behind Umm Salamah's famous name is both interesting and heart-breaking. Before her marriage to the Prophet ﷺ, she was married to Abū Salamah ﵁, who was a faithful and close Companion to the Prophet ﷺ. A son was born to them after migration, whom they named 'Salamah', hence their shared names. Their marriage was a blessed one, with immense happiness, love, and compassion. However, life took an unforeseen turn when Abū Salamah ؓ got sick and passed away, leaving her a widow. But something interesting happened before his death. The Prophet ﷺ taught them what to say when dealing with a loss.

Umm Salamah ؓ reported: 'I heard the Messenger of Allah ﷺ saying, "When a person suffers from a calamity and utters:

'We belong to Allah and to Him we shall return. O Allah! Compensate me in my affliction, recompense my loss, and give me something better in exchange for it', then Allah surely compensates him with a reward and a better substitute."'

(Muslim)

Losing a loved one is a huge calamity and tests a person in the most extreme way. It is a phase in which a person goes through a lot of emotions and feelings of loss, and this was exactly how Sayyidah Umm Salamah ؓ felt. She was heartbroken, but she also was not sure how this supplication would help her. Abū Salamah ؓ was a loving husband, an adoring father, and a noble human being. She could not imagine any other person who could fill his place in a better way. She was unsure, yet her faith in the words of Allah ﷻ made her repeat this supplication again and again. And Allah ﷻ blessed her with a companion better than she could have ever imagined: the Messenger of Allah ﷺ himself.

This is where we see the profound wisdom of Umm Salamah ؓ and her foresight. When the proposal came to her from the

Prophet ﷺ, she knew that her position as a widow and a mother was delicate. She was aware of her weaknesses and wanted to assess the situation carefully, and thus, took her time before replying. She sent a message to the Prophet ﷺ, saying, 'Tell him that I am a woman on the older side, and I am a woman with many children, and I am someone who is jealous by nature.' She was in her thirties at this point. She wanted to be transparent about her realities and expectations and was telling him that she may not be easy to live with or give him what he wanted. The Prophet ﷺ, however, had a generous heart full of compassion and kindness. He sent a reply to her in a wise manner and said, 'Tell her that if she is old, I am older. If she has children and she is worried about them, I will supplicate to Allah ﷻ to take care of her children. And regarding the feeling of jealousy she has, I will also supplicate to Allah ﷻ to remove it from her heart.' She thus accepted the proposal, and they were married.

Blessed with Beauty, Wisdom, and Bravery

Umm Salamah رضي الله عنها was not only blessed with physical beauty but she was also endowed a sharp intellect. She was born into a noble family and was among the few women of her time who memorised and narrated the Hadiths of the Prophet Muhammad ﷺ. Major Companions, including the great Companion Sayyidunā 'Abdullāh ibn 'Abbās رضي الله عنهما, sought her counsel, a testament to her wisdom. One of the reasons for why she is described as wise is because when the Prophet ﷺ proposed to her, she took her time and thought about it. She neither got carried away by emotions and said yes right away nor made a hasty decision to say no. She understood that she had to come to terms with certain things about herself and work on herself before saying yes. And this was her gift, her foresightedness, and insight as she fully accepted the responsibility of becoming the Prophet's wife.

Umm Salamah ﵂ was also very brave and fought with the Prophet ﷺ in four battles in Medina, taking position at the forefront of the army.

A Legacy of Sound Counsel

Umm Salamah's wisdom shone brightest during the Treaty of Ḥudaybiyyah, a pivotal moment in Islamic history. This treaty took place when the Muslims left Medina with the intention of performing 'Umrah but they were stopped by the Quraysh, and instead, a treaty was signed between their ambassador and the Prophet ﷺ. However, the treaty was largely in favour of the Quraysh and appeared to be prejudiced against the Muslims; it stated that the Muslims would not get to perform 'Umrah this year and would have to come back next year. The conditions of the treaty, along with the helplessness of the Muslims in iḥrām (the sacred state to perform pilgrimage), was too much for them to take. They were inconsolable to the point that Sayyidunā 'Umar ﵁ came to the Prophet ﷺ and said, 'O Messenger of Allah, why are we accepting this? Are we not on the right path?' They were unaware of it, but Allah ﷻ had a better plan. The wisdom behind this seemingly disastrous event was far greater and would impact the course of Islamic history. Believing in the plan of Allah ﷻ, the Prophet ﷺ signed the treaty, knowing that it would bring only goodness and benefit. But they were now in a predicament. The Companions were in iḥrām, and since they could not perform

'Umrah, they had to take it off. This meant changing, shaving off their hair, and sacrificing the animals they brought along. The Prophet ﷺ was respected and revered to such a level that when he used to make his ablution, the Companions would put their hands under him to collect the water out of love and obedience. Expecting the same love and obedience from them, the Prophet ﷺ looked at the Companions and said, 'Take off your iḥrām and shave your heads.' No one moved. He said it again. No one moved. He said it the third time. Still, no one moved. The Prophet ﷺ, anguished by their lack of response, turned and went to his tent.

What happened next is the shining example of Umm Salamah's timely advice and sharp thinking. When the Prophet ﷺ related to her what had happened outside with the Companions, she advised him to not do anything and just go out without saying a word. He should take off his iḥrām, shave his head, and see what the Companions do. She insisted that they would all follow him, and that was exactly what happened. The Prophet ﷺ went out and began to remove his iḥrām without saying a word to anyone, and the Companions followed. It was as if they finally accepted the decree of Allah ﷻ by seeing the Prophet ﷺ. Simple advice by a woman with foresight and wisdom was able to dissolve this tense situation and help everyone come to terms with reality.

This was perhaps one of her most admirable qualities, as the Qur'an says:

'And whoever is granted wisdom is certainly blessed with a great privilege.'

(al-Baqarah, 2:269)

Inspiring Revelation in the Name of Women

Umm Salamah migrated twice, being one of the first women to migrate to Medina and Abyssinia on two separate occasions. Just like Sayyidah ʿĀ'ishah, her defining quality was her knowledge, intellect and ability to make informed decisions. Moreover, she too, like Sayyidah ʿĀ'ishah, was in the habit of asking questions regarding the Islamic message. This was to the extent that three verses of the Qur'an were revealed due to a question she asked the Prophet ﷺ. She said, 'O Messenger of Allah, the men take all the rewards, the men go out for jihad and we do not do that.' She said, 'Why are men mentioned in the Qur'an, and we are not mentioned?' Allah revealed the following verse of Sūrah al-Aḥzāb to answer her queries:

'Surely Muslim men and women, believing men and women, devout men and women, truthful men and women, patient men and women, humble men and women, charitable men and women, fasting men and women, men and women who guard their chastity, and men and women who remember Allah often – for all of them Allah has prepared forgiveness and a great reward.'

(al-Aḥzāb, 33:35)

This unique verse puts the hearts of all at ease and clearly mentions that those who are believing, devout, truthful, patient, humble, charitable, modest, and fearful of Allah will have equal rewards, regardless of whether they are men or women. Whoever does a good deed will have it rewarded and whoever does a sin will find its punishment.

In a verse from another sūrah of the Qur'an, Allah says:

مَنْ عَمِلَ صَـٰلِحًا مِّن ذَكَرٍ أَوْ أُنثَىٰ وَهُوَ مُؤْمِنٌ فَلَنُحْيِيَنَّهُۥ حَيَوٰةً طَيِّبَةً ۖ وَلَنَجْزِيَنَّهُمْ أَجْرَهُم بِأَحْسَنِ مَا كَانُوا۟ يَعْمَلُونَ

'Whoever does good, whether male or female, and is a believer, We will surely bless them with a good life, and We will certainly reward them according to the best of their deeds.'

(al-Naḥl, 16:97)

Her question was answered by the Highest and most Supreme Being, Allah ﷻ. She voiced the concern of all those women who were silently looking for this answer. Allah ﷻ listened to her and sent down a revelation to address her concern. What a great honour!

Her contributions also include one of the Hadiths narrated by her that we know today and read in our daily supplications.

اللَّهمَّ إنِّي أسأَلُكَ عِلمًا نافعًا، ورِزْقًا طيِّبًا، وعمَلًا مُتقَبَّلًا

'O God, I ask You for beneficial knowledge, acceptable action, and good provision.'

(Ibn Mājah)

This supplication is a comprehensive and wholesome prayer for everything we need to live a good life. What does a person need in life to be happy and content? Knowledge to make the right decisions, a good income and provision, and good actions to reach the ultimate destination, Jannah. And this supplication encompasses all those elements. She learned this supplication from the Prophet ﷺ, as he used to read it at the time of Fajr. What a beautiful contribution for the Ummah. Umm Salamah ؓ narrated more than 300 Hadiths, including the aforementioned one.

The Last Days

Umm Salamah was the laŝt wife of the Prophet to die during the time of Yazīd ibn Muʿāwiyah. Sayyidunā Abu Hurayrah prayed the janāzah over her and she was buried in al-Baqīʿ in Medina. Umm Salamah's remarkable qualities, wisdom, courage, and honeŝty have left an enduring legacy for all Muslims to follow. Her commitment to seeking knowledge, truŝting in the plan of Allah, and asking for beneficial suŝtenance serve as an inspiration for us all.

CHAPTER SEVEN

Zaynab bint Jaḥsh ﷺ

The history of Islam is rich with stories of women who contributed to the building of a nation through their unique characters and qualities. They participated in its victory with their generosity, determination, and steadfastness. Of these was Sayyidah Zaynab bint Jaḥsh. She was a remarkable woman and a relative of the Prophet Muhammad ﷺ. Her mother was the aunt of the Prophet ﷺ, and her family consisted of high-ranking Companions, including her sisters. Sayyidah Zaynab bint Jaḥsh possessed several unique qualities that set her apart from others.

The Reward of Obedience

Sayyidah Zaynab bint Jaḥsh was extremely beautiful and was well known for her splendour. She was very pious and generous, famous for her benevolence and charitable deeds. She was quite unique in her personality, as she was also a business woman. But this was not the only unique aspect about her work. The income from her business was given in donations to help the poor and needy.

Allah tests us in different ways and her test was quite unique. She had a privileged upbringing, belonging to a noble family, and was blessed with both beauty and status. Many proposals came for her but Allah ﷻ had other plans. The Prophet ﷺ wanted her to marry Zayd ibn Ḥārithah ﷺ, his adopted son. At the time, he was called by the name Zayd ibn Muhammad, which was later changed according to an Islamic ruling. However, Zaynab and her family were not happy with the proposal, as they felt he was not a suitable match for her. However, Allah ﷻ revealed a verse in Sūrah al-Aḥzāb addressing the decision for Sayyidah Zaynab ﷺ to marry Zayd. Allah ﷻ says:

'It is not for a believing man or woman – when Allah and His Messenger decree a matter – to have any other choice in that matter.'

(al-Aḥzāb, 33:35)

When she heard this verse, she obeyed Allah's decree and the Prophet's order, and the marriage took place. However, the marriage did not last long, and they were divorced within a year. Allah ﷻ rewarded Zaynab for obeying Him by marrying her to the Prophet ﷺ. There were many unique aspects to this marriage; not only did Zaynab go from being hesitantly married to the Prophet's adopted son to being divorced in such a short span of time and then married to the Prophet ﷺ himself, but it was Allah ﷻ Who ordained both marriages. Allah ﷻ says in the 37th verse of the same sūrah: 'We married her to you.' Some scholars even say that the Qur'an was the witness to their marriage.

A Beautiful Bond

From the wives of the Prophet 🌸, there were two who were the closest to him. One of them was Zaynab 🌸, and the other, as previously mentioned, was Sayyidah ʿĀʾishah 🌸. Both women were also close to one another, and a test that Sayyidah ʿĀʾishah 🌸 went through gives a clear example of their bond and highlights the honesty and justness of Sayyidah Zaynab 🌸.

The slander incident against ʿĀʾishah was a tumultuous time for both her and the Prophet 🌸. However, it also brought forward the noble qualities of the Companions around him, just as it shone light on the nobility of Sayyidah Zaynab's character. When the Prophet 🌸 came to Sayyidah Zaynab 🌸 before ʿĀʾishah's innocence was revealed and asked her, 'What do you think of ʿĀʾishah?' she said, 'I am not going to say anything that my ear did not hear or my eyes did not see. I do not know anything but good about her.' In this response, Zaynab exemplified integrity and justice. She did not go along with the gossip and rumours to take advantage of the situation and tarnish the image of Sayyidah ʿĀʾishah 🌸. Instead, she defended her and said kind words about her, reinforcing the belief of the Prophet 🌸 in Sayyidah ʿĀʾishah 🌸.

Similarly, Sayyidah ʿĀʾishah 🌸 also had only good words to say about Zaynab. She said, 'I have never seen a woman who is more conscious of Allah 🌸, who does acts of worship as much as she does, who is as keen about the relationship with her family, and as generous and just as Zaynab.' The strange thing is that they were not sisters, not even friends, but they were instead the wives of the Prophet 🌸. Their bond was free of any malice or jealousy and was one that was full of mutual respect and compassion.

Generosity and Exemplary Worship

Sayyidah Zaynab's generousity was very well known. She had a workshop where leather was made, and the sales from it were donated completely to the poor, earning her the title of 'The Mother of the Poor and Needy' (Umm al-Masākīn). She was also very pious and God-fearing and had kept a special place in her home for the worship of Allah ﷻ. She was known to stand long hours in ṣalāh, reading the Qur'an. Her beautiful example is something that we can all follow by making our own place or corner of worship in our house where we can pray, supplicate, and contemplate upon the Qur'an.

It is reported that she died at the age of 53 or 54 and had prepared her own shroud, exemplifying her longing to meet Allah ﷻ. It is a well-documented fact that she had asked for a screen to be put up so no one could see her body even when shrouded, displaying her high level of modesty and fear of Allah ﷻ. She was buried in al-Baqīʿ, Medina.

Sayyidah Zaynab ﵂ serves as a shining example of a builder of a nation. Her beauty, piety, generosity, humility, and devotion to Allah ﷻ and His Prophet ﷺ render her a role model for all Muslims.

CHAPTER EIGHT

Juwayriyyah bint al-Ḥārith ﵂

Every person wishes to have a life of luxury and privilege, but no matter what blessings we have, everything is temporary. We may face many ups and downs but how we deal with these situations is what makes or breaks us. The life of Juwayriyyah bint al-Ḥārith ﵂ presents the account of a legendary woman of Islam who went through similar ups and downs, taking her from the status of a princess to the position of a prisoner of war. Her faith and exemplary character made her a builder of a nation, keeping her alive in our memories as one of the noble wives of the Prophet ﷺ.

From Tragedy to Faith

Sayyidah Juwayriyyah bint al-Ḥārith ﵂ was the daughter of the leader of Khuzāʿah, a well-known tribe in Medina, and her father al-Ḥārith was the leader. Raised as a princess, she lived in luxury and nobility. When the Prophet ﷺ came to know that Khuzāʿah was planning to attack the Muslims, instead of waiting for them to attack, he went out of Medina to a place called al-Sarīʿ,

which is a spring of water. There, the Muslims met Khuzāʿah and defeated them.

This was the point where the life of Sayyidah Juwayriyyah bint al-Ḥārith ؓ changed drastically. Prior to the battle, Juwayriyyah had a dream in which she saw the moon falling into her lap. She felt good about the dream and knew something unique was going to happen in her life. However, during the attack, her husband was killed and she was taken as a captive of war, which was very common during these times. After the war, she fell under the care of Thābit ibn al-Qays ؓ, and as was the custom at the time, she asked Thābit to write a contract for her release. As a princess, well-regarded, and accustomed to luxury, Sayyidah Juwayriyyah bint al-Ḥārith ؓ felt deeply uncomfortable and embarrassed with the situation and so she reached out to the Prophet ﷺ to intervene. Even though the Prophet ﷺ was the same person who attacked her tribe and resulted in her present condition, she exhibited great intelligence and deep insight, and with the utmost respect for him, asked for his assistance.

She said to the Prophet ﷺ, 'O Prophet of Allah, I am the daughter of al-Ḥārith ibn Abī Ḍirār, who is the leader of his people. Surely, you know the calamity I went through. I became a widow, got captured, and left my family. And I asked Qays, the one under whose care I am, to write a contract for me, but I want you to help me. I want you to release me and write the contract.' The Prophet ﷺ gave her two options: she could either be freed and return to her family, or he would marry her and secure her release. Sayyidah Juwayriyyah ؓ gladly accepted the latter option, as she understood that this was what her dream implied. Her marriage to the Prophet ﷺ brought immense blessings to her people and tribe, as many were released from captivity and many embraced Islam due to her union with the Prophet ﷺ.

Nobility and Grace

Her description, as told by Sayyidah ʿĀ'ishah ؓ, makes one feel in awe of her, with her beauty described as breath-taking. She said, 'Her beauty was like a fairy tale.' She was not just elegant and graceful due to her luxurious lifestyle but also had nobility embedded in her character. Along with these physical attributes, she was also very intelligent and wise and had mastered many languages. But the biggest gift of Allah ﷻ to her was that she was blessed with the position any woman would dream of – as the Companion of the Prophet ﷺ and the mother of all believers.

Before her marriage with the Prophet ﷺ, her name was Barra, which is derived from the Arabic word 'بر', which means excellence. But the Prophet ﷺ changed it to Juwayriyyah, as it is disliked in Islam to give names that praise oneself. Sayyidah Juwayriyyah ؓ was described by Sayyidah ʿĀ'ishah ؓ in the following words: 'I have not seen a person who brought so many blessings to her family like Juwayriyyah.' Because of her marriage to the Prophet ﷺ, all the Companions in Medina who were captured were set free. In addition to this, her father, the leader of the Khuzāʿah tribe, became Muslim. As a result of this, many people of Khuzāʿah also became Muslims.

A Virtuous Choice

Sayyidah Juwayriyyah was presented with a choice that would change the course of her life and define who she became. Before she married the Prophet ﷺ, her father came to her and offered to free her from captivity by paying the amount required. However, her heart was set, and she responded with confidence, 'I have chosen Allah ﷻ and His Messenger ﷺ.' The decision between faith and the luxuries of life was a defining moment for her, taking her from disbelief to belief in the Only One Truth, Allah ﷻ. This serves as a lesson to us to always keep Allah ﷻ first, and always choose Him over everything.

Sayyidah Juwayriyyah was also unique in her devoutness and worship. She stood for hours in worship, remembering and supplicating to Allah ﷻ. In a Hadith narrated by Imam Muslim, she prayed Fajr and remained seated in her place, remembering Allah ﷻ. When the Prophet ﷺ left for Fajr and returned after Ḍuḥā, he found Juwayriyyah sitting in the same place, supplicating and remembering Allah ﷻ. He ﷺ looked at her and said, 'You are still in the same position as I left you?' She said, 'Yes.' In response, he said to her, 'I am going to teach you something.' He taught her the following supplication:

سُبْحَانَ اللهِ وَبِحَمْدِهِ، عَدَدَ خَلْقِهِ، وَرِضَا نَفْسِهِ، وَزِنَةَ عَرْشِهِ وَمِدَادَ كَلِمَاتِهِ

'Allah is free from imperfection and I begin with His praise, as many times as the number of His creatures, in accordance with His Good Pleasure, equal to the weight of His Throne and equal to the ink that may be used in recording the words (for His Praise).'

(al-Bukhārī)

He ﷺ told her that if she said these four phrases three times in the morning, they would weigh far more than all the hours she had spent sitting in the remembrance of Allah ﷻ. This supplication is now a part of our morning and evening supplication routine. Sayyidah Juwayriyyah became a source of this blessing for the entire ummah, as it was her action and dedicated worship that taught us these beneficial words.

Ruling on Friday Fasting

Sayyidah Juwayriyyah's example also influenced the ruling of fasting on Fridays. When the Prophet ﷺ found her fasting on a Friday without fasting the day before or after, he advised her to break her fast, as narrated by Imam al-Bukhārī. From this, we understand that it is disliked singling out Fridays for fasting without fasting on Thursday or Saturday, unless there is an acceptable reason.

Sayyidah Juwayriyyah died 56 years after the Hijrah at the age of 65, at the same time as Muʿāwiyah. She was buried in al-Baqīʿ in Medina, and the funeral prayer for her was led by the governor of Medina, Marwān ibn al-Ḥakam.

ṢAFIYYAH BINT ḤUYAYY رضي الله عنها

By Allah عز وجل, the Prophet ﷺ and Islam is more beloved to me than Judaism and my family.

CHAPTER NINE

Ṣafiyyah bint Ḥuyayy ﵂

Among the luminous figures who shaped the fabric of our ummah and contributed to the foundation of our faith, there are unique women whose stories illuminate the path of our journey. These women, whose lives intertwine with the legacy of the Prophet Muhammad ﷺ and the birth of Islam, embody courage, devotion, and resilience. We now encounter another legendary figure, Sayyidah Ṣafiyyah bint Ḥuyayy ﵂, a woman of remarkable depth and strength.

From Judaism to Islam

Sayyidah Ṣafiyyah bint Ḥuyayy ﵂ was born into a Jewish family in the Jewish Banū Naḍīr tribe of Medina. As the daughter of the leader of Banū Naḍīr, she enjoyed many luxuries and privileges. Eventually her life unfolded in a series of transformative events that brought her towards Islam. Sayyidah Ṣafiyyah ﵂ was described by Umm Sulaym ﵂ as extremely beautiful. She was very intelligent and generous and frequently gave money to her family and the poor. Sayyidah Ṣafiyyah ﵂ was married twice before her marriage with the Prophet ﷺ. The first marriage ended in divorce and the second left her widowed.

As the clouds of conflict gathered over Medina, Ṣafiyyah's tribe got expelled to the outskirts of the city. Here, Ṣafiyyah's life took a tumultuous turn: she was forced to leave home, both her father and husband were killed in one of the battles with Banū Naḍīr, and she was taken by the Muslims as a captive of war. She now found herself in a testing situation, for she went from being the daughter of a leader to a captive of war, widowed and away from home. This was indeed a difficult test, but one which she faced with true courage and strength of faith.

When the Prophet ﷺ offered to marry Ṣafiyyah, he gave her a choice. He said to her, 'O Ṣafiyyah, you came from a noble family and you still have some of your family on the outskirts of Medina. If you wish, I will set you free and you can go back to your family. Or if you wish, I will marry you and you will be one of the mothers of the believers.' A choice lay before Sayyidah Ṣafiyyah ؓ – to return to her family or marry the Prophet ﷺ – and her decision reflected her faith's transformational power. She said, 'O Prophet of Islam, I admire Islam, and I admired you before you called me to be a wife or to be a Muslim. I have no interest in Judaism and I have no father or brother to go back to. If you give me the choice between Judaism and freedom as opposed to Islam, I am not going to choose anything but Islam. And by Allah, the Prophet ﷺ and Islam is more beloved to me than Judaism and my family.'

The marriage proposal of the Prophet ﷺ at this time was a blessing and behind their union lay great wisdom; not only would this marriage bring the tribes of Medina together but it would also bring back Ṣafiyyah's honour as the daughter of a tribal leader.

Challenges of Faith

Sayyidah Ṣafiyyah's marriage to the Prophet ﷺ was marked by challenges, particularly arising from the jealousy of other wives, including Sayyidah ʿĀ'ishah ؓ and Sayyidah Zaynab ؓ. Often adamant about declaring their unacceptance, they found it difficult to accept Ṣafiyyah because of her Jewish background and the fact that her father was one of the main enemies of the Prophet ﷺ. Sayyidah Ṣafiyyah ؓ was questioned about her sincerity in faith and indirectly accused of still being Jewish.

Sayyidah Ṣafiyyah ؓ also prepared delicious meals – a trait that made Sayyidah ʿĀ'ishah ؓ jealous. Narrations speak of an occasion where Ṣafiyyah cooked a meal and sent it to the Prophet ﷺ. As the Prophet ﷺ entered the house carrying the dish, Sayyidah ʿĀ'ishah ؓ made a point to break it and admitted this was out of jealousy. The Prophet ﷺ was upset. ʿĀ'ishah asked how she might make up for this, and the Prophet ﷺ told her to get the same dish, cook it, and send it back to Ṣafiyyah. On another occasion, the Prophet ﷺ was speaking of Sayyidah Ṣafiyyah ؓ, and Sayyidah ʿĀ'ishah ؓ disliked it to the extent that she said something about Ṣafiyyah's height being short. This upset the Prophet ﷺ deeply, and he expressed his displeasure to Sayyidah ʿĀ'ishah ؓ, saying, 'You have said a word that, if mixed with the water of the sea, the sea would be polluted.' It was a lesson to Sayyidah ʿĀ'ishah ؓ, just as it is a lesson to us, to refrain from calling names or belittling someone. It is highly disliked to mock someone using their description or physical appearance, even if it is true, as it can hurt the person and make them feel devoid of value.

Sayyidah Ḥafṣah bint ʿUmar 🙵 also had difficulty accepting Sayyidah Ṣafiyyah 🙵 and was reported to have referred to her as Jewish. On one occasion, the Prophet 🙵 found Sayyidah Ṣafiyyah 🙵 crying because of what the other wives called her. Referring to Prophet Mūsā 🙵, Prophet Hārūn 🙵, and himself, the Prophet 🙵 asked her to go back and tell them, 'My father is a Prophet, my uncle is a Prophet, and my husband is a Prophet, so why do you think you are better than me?'

A Hajj Legacy

Sayyidah Ṣafiyyah 🙵 conferred a huge favour for the women of our ummah, as it was due to her that we find one of the rulings of Hajj related to menstruating women. Sayyidah Ṣafiyyah 🙵 was performing Hajj with the Prophet 🙵. It was the last day, and they were planning to go back to Medina after completing the farewell ṭawāf (circumambulation) around the Kaʿbah. However, the Prophet 🙵 was informed that Ṣafiyyah had not completed the farewell ṭawāf due to her menstruating. The Prophet 🙵 said, 'If she is menstruating, then the farewell ṭawāf is not an obligation on her, and we can leave.' At this point, the ruling was established that if a woman is menstruating, the farewell ṭawāf is not an obligation for her.

A Loyal and a Generous Spirit

Sayyidah Ṣafiyyah 🙵 was a noble woman who went through challenges and tests for her love of Islam. Her heart was sincere and full of love for the Prophet 🙵, so much so that when he was sick in his final days, she looked at him and said, 'I wish that your suffering is given to me and you will be free and healthy of any pain and any suffering.' When she said this, the wives of the Prophet ﷺ looked at each other, and the Prophet ﷺ looked at them and said, 'By Allah, I know Ṣafiyyah is truthful and loyal and she meant what she said.'

She was extremely generous and donated all her wealth to the poor and needy, and even supported her family. She passed away in Medina 52 years after the Hijrah at the age of 60, during the reign of Muʿāwiyah. She was also buried in al-Baqīʿ.

Sayyidah Ṣafiyyah's journey offers invaluable lessons for navigating the challenges of faith, identity, and community. Sayyidah Ṣafiyyah embraced transformation, and her ability to change adversity into strength, her unwavering commitment to Islam, and her exemplary conduct inspire believers to emulate her noble traits.

CHAPTER TEN

Ramlah bint Abī Sufyān ﵅

When it comes to our status in the sight of Allah ﷻ, what matters is our faith and actions. This is why the daughter of Abū Sufyān, the leader of Quraysh and one of the fiercest enemies of Islam, did not just become a Muslim but was also honoured with being the wife of the Prophet ﷺ. The journey of Ramlah bint Abī Sufyān or Umm Ḥabībah ﵅ and how she went from being the daughter of a staunch enemy of the Prophet ﷺ to becoming one of his wives is an extraordinary story that echoes the triumph of faith over prejudice and the power of a woman's conviction.

A Transformative Journey of Faith

Sayyidah Umm Ḥabībah ﵅ was one of the earliest women to accept Islam. Her husband, ʿUbaydullāh ibn Jaḥsh, the brother of Sayyidah Zaynab bint Jaḥsh ﵅, also accepted Islam. She was brave enough to declare her faith while her father was an open and powerful enemy of Islam, and leaving behind everything, she migrated with her husband to Abyssinia. Afterwards, her husband rejected Islam and converted to Christianity, forcing her to do the same. Soon after, he died, leaving Sayyidah Umm Ḥabībah a widow with a baby girl named Ḥabībah. Sayyidah Umm Ḥabībah

رضي الله عنها was left in a difficult situation as a single mother in a foreign land with no support and no one to rely on other than Allah ﷻ.

As she was known to have dreams that came true, it was only natural that Sayyidah Umm Ḥabībah رضي الله عنها had a dream regarding her marriage to the Prophet ﷺ. She said, 'I heard someone in my dream saying to me, "Mother of the faithful."' Since she knew that this title was only given to the wives of the Prophet ﷺ, she understood that she was going to marry him soon. And sure enough, upon hearing of her situation and in a noble gesture to honour her integrity and wellbeing, the Prophet ﷺ asked for her hand in marriage. When the proposal reached her, her happiness knew no bounds.

The marriage took place under the guardianship of al-Najāshī, and even though the Prophet ﷺ was in Mecca, al-Najāshī made sure that the celebration of the marriage was conducted suitably, with all guests eating, drinking, and feeling welcomed, as was the Sunnah. Al-Najāshī's hospitality and generosity exemplified his love and respect for the Prophet ﷺ. Sayyidah Umm Ḥabībah رضي الله عنها was also given gifts by the wives of al-Najāshī and, in return, she offered gifts to those who attended the wedding and took care of her. This was a dream come true, and with a heart content and happy with the blessing of Allah, she gave generously!

Sayyidah Umm Ḥabībah's father was still a disbeliever and staunch enemy of Islam, but when he received news of his daughter's marriage with the Prophet of Allah ﷻ, he was happy. It seems strange that he would approve of this union while opposing the message of Islam, but when we read a particular verse that Allah ﷻ revealed in Sūrah al-Mumtaḥanah, we begin to understand His grand plan.

Allah ﷻ says:

عَسَى ٱللَّهُ أَن يَجْعَلَ بَيْنَكُمْ وَبَيْنَ ٱلَّذِينَ عَادَيْتُم مِّنْهُم مَّوَدَّةً وَٱللَّهُ قَدِيرٌ وَٱللَّهُ غَفُورٌ رَّحِيمٌ

'Allah may bring about goodwill between you and those of them you hold as enemies. For Allah is Most Capable. And Allah is All-Forgiving, Most Merciful.'

(al-Mumtaḥanah, 60:7)

Umm Ḥabībah ؓ migrated to Medina along with the Prophet ﷺ and lived a happy and fulfilling life. Her character shone brightly through her actions and demeanour. She loved the Prophet ﷺ immensely, and her respect and reverence for him is evident from an incident that happened with her father before he accepted Islam. Abū Sufyān visited her once in Medina, hoping for her intervention between the Prophet ﷺ and him in a matter. When he entered and proceeded to sit on a couch that had a blanket on it, she removed the blanket and stopped him from sitting there, telling him confidently that it was the place for the Prophet ﷺ and that he was not fit to sit in the same place as the noblest and purest man, the Messenger of Allah ﷺ. She exhibited exceptional confidence and conviction in her faith and stood by the truth in front of her father because of his rejection of Islam. This was the courageous character of Sayyidah Umm Ḥabībah ؓ, a noble woman indeed.

After 10 years filled with tests, her patience and steadfastness did not go unrewarded. Abū Sufyān, her father, accepted Islam at the time of the conquest of Mecca in the 10th Hijri year.

An Asset to the Community

Sayyidah Umm Ḥabībah ❀ was very knowledgeable. She was the third highest female narrator of Hadiths, narrating 60 Hadiths in total. One of her most valuable contributions was the Hadith she reported concerning the virtues of praying 12 extra units of Sunnah prayer, which consist of the following: two before Fajr, four or two before Ẓuhr, four or two after Ẓuhr, two after Maghrib, and two after Ishā'. It is mentioned in the Hadith that the reward for the one performing these units is that Allah ❀ will build a house in Jannah for them.

Sayyidah Umm Ḥabībah's knowledge served as an asset for the ummah and it was through her that we also find a pivotal ruling of fiqh. When her father died and the news came to her, she made it a point to make it public and put on perfume after the third day. She addressed the people and said, 'I do not need to put on perfume, but I have heard the Prophet ❀ say that a woman is not allowed to mourn for any member of her family other than her husband for more than three days and for her husband four months and ten days.' As a result of this, this ruling has now become a legislation.

Humble and Courageous

The nobility of Sayyidah Umm Ḥabībah's character can also be seen from an incident where she asked Sayyidah Umm Salamah ❀ for forgiveness. Sayyidah Umm Ḥabībah ❀ said, 'There was something between you and me, and as I am departing, I want you to forgive me. I have already forgiven you.' Sayyidah Umm

Salamah replied, 'I want you to forgive me, and I have already forgiven you.' These were the women who carried the legacy of Islam and left an example for the future generations with their generous spirit and pure hearts.

Sayyidah Umm Ḥabībah has a special place in the history of Islam for her unwavering faith and courage. Her story reminds us that faith can transform lives, heal relationships, and provide the strength to navigate even the most difficult trials. She remained brave even when her husband rejected Islam and forced her to do the same, staying firm on the religion and managing herself as a widow and a single mother in a strange land all by herself. Her only solace was relying on Allah and believing in her heart that He would never let her down.

Sayyidah Umm Ḥabībah died 44 years after the migration to Medina at the time of the leadership of her brother Muʿāwiyah. She remained courageous and steadfast until her last moments.

CHAPTER ELEVEN

Maymūnah bint al-Ḥārith رضي الله عنها

There were some women in the history of Islam whose choices continued to have an impact for generations after they departed this world, leaving a legacy of virtues and lessons behind them. Amongst such women was the virtuous figure Maymūnah bint al-Ḥārith رضي الله عنها, a unique woman whose choices kept her name alive as a mother of the believers.

Distinguished by Family and Character

Sayyidah Maymūnah bint al-Ḥārith رضي الله عنها was born and brought up in a noble family in Mecca. Her name was originally Barrah, but it was changed to Maymūnah after she married the Prophet ﷺ. Her new name was chosen by the Prophet ﷺ and means blessings or a woman who brings blessing.

Her sister, Lubābah رضي الله عنها, was the second woman to accept Islam and her half-sister, Sayyidah Zaynab bint Khuzaymah رضي الله عنها, was also one of the wives of the Prophet ﷺ. Sayyidah Maymūnah رضي الله عنها was the aunt of two of the biggest icons of the Muslim ummah, Sayyidunā Khālid ibn al-Walīd and ʿAbdullāh ibn ʿAbbās رضي الله عنهما. She embraced Islam before the Hijrah and stayed in Mecca until she moved to Medina three years after her marriage to the Prophet ﷺ.

Described as someone who was very pious and by the Prophet ﷺ as 'a symbol of goodness', Sayyidah Maymūnah's characteristics and attributes were just as distinctive as her familial relations. Uniquely, she was known for her confidence and proactive nature. An example of this can be seen in her proposing marriage to the Prophet ﷺ. It is reported that she either sent a relative or the husband of her sister to propose to the Prophet ﷺ or proposed to him directly when they were in a caravan. Her decision to propose marriage set her apart as a woman who was proactive in shaping her destiny and underscores the importance of taking initiative. She wanted to be a mother of the believers, a position of utmost honour and blessing!

A Legacy of Knowledge

Sayyidah Maymūnah ؓ was one of the authorities of fiqh, and this was her legacy for the future generations. Her knowledge and teachings provide guidance on various aspects of religious practice and daily life. Many of the sayings of the Prophet ﷺ related to fiqh rulings, such as the rulings of how to perform things in Islam, were narrated by Sayyidah Maymūnah ؓ. An example of this is the ruling regarding the Islamic bath, which is known as ghusl. Sayyidah Maymūnah ؓ said that she would prepare the water for the Prophet ﷺ and went on to describe exactly what he did. She not only described the necessary basics of the Islamic bath, but also reported the Sunnah acts that the Prophet ﷺ engaged in.

Sayyidah Maymūnah ؓ also narrated a Hadith regarding the virtues of the Mosque of the Prophet ﷺ. There was a woman in Medina who was ill. She said that if Allah ﷻ cured her, she would go and pray in Masjid al-Aqṣā in Jerusalem. She told Sayyidah Maymūnah about this, and when Allah ﷻ cured her, Sayyidah Maymūnah gave her sound advice. She told her to stay there and eat from the food she made and pray in the Mosque of the Prophet ﷺ. She told her that she heard the Prophet ﷺ saying that praying in his Mosque is a thousand times better than praying in any other mosque, save al-Bayt al-Ḥarām – which is the mosque in Mecca.

One of the most important rulings that Sayyidah Maymūnah narrated was a ruling related to Hajj. While the Prophet ﷺ stood supplicating on the day of ʿArafah, people wanted to know whether he was fasting or not. Out of awe and respect for him, they could not ask him this directly. Sayyidah Maymūnah was both wise and considerate of others, so she did something brilliant. She handed him a glass of milk, and when he drank it, their doubts were cleared. The ruling was thus established that those present in ʿArafah at the time of Hajj need not fast. This incident again exhibited her brilliance and consideration for the Prophet ﷺ and shone light on an important aspect of Islam.

An Affectionate Heart

Another of Sayyidah Maymūnah's unique and exceptional qualities was her considerate and affectionate nature. On one occasion, she was sitting with the Prophet ﷺ and Sayyidunā Khālid ibn al-Walīd and her brother-in-law, al-Faḍl, who had brought meat with them. She knew that the Prophet ﷺ refrained from certain foods out of preference, so when he was about to pick up a piece of meat, she informed him that it was the meat of a lizard. The

Prophet ﷺ put it back and said that he did not eat such meat, and told the Companions to go ahead and eat it. She exhibited thoughtfulness by informing him about it, and even though the Companions ate the food, she refrained out of her love for the Prophet ﷺ and not wanting to eat something that her husband and the Prophet of Allah ﷺ did not like to eat. Unsuitable for his own palette, his choice not to eat lizard meat showed his human nature and did not constitute a ruling against it.

Sayyidah Maymūnah passed away in the 61st year after the Hijrah. Interestingly, she was not buried in al-Baqīʿ. Instead, her resting place is in Saraf, which lies at the outskirts of Mecca. Sayyidah ʿĀ'ishah said about her, 'There is no more Maymūnah. By Allah, she was the most pious among us and she was the most caring of her relatives.' Her death marked the conclusion of a life dedicated to faith, knowledge, and service.

Her funeral was attended by her family, including ʿAbdullāh ibn ʿAbbās, the Most Knowledgeable Man of Islam (Ḥabr al-Ummah). From her initial days in Mecca to her revered status as one of the Mothers of the Believers, her life is a testament to the boundless mercy and blessings that accompany the path of Islam.

CHAPTER THIRTEEN

Māriyyah bint Shamʿūn ﵂

One of the beauties of our religion is how it transcends cultures and nations and binds people together with faith irrespective of where they came from or what they believed in before encountering Islam. This is the story of a remarkable woman, Sayyidah Māriyyah al-Qibṭiyyah ﵂, whose presence in the history of Islam is unique from various perspectives. Hers is a narrative filled with cultural diversity, faith transformation, and profound emotional experience.

Inclined Toward the Truth

Quite distinctively, Sayyidah Māriyyah al-Qibṭiyyah ﵂ was an Egyptian Christian or Egyptian Coptic who lived in Egypt. She was not a free woman but a slave who was serving the governor of Alexandria along with her sister. After the seventh year of the Hijrah and the signing of the Treaty of Ḥudaybiyyah, the Prophet ﷺ began sending letters to the neighbouring countries to invite them to Islam, as was a common custom at the time. In return, governors of those countries would send gifts, and even though this is not uncommon in today's time, the gifts they sent were different from now. They would send slaves, and so Sayyidah Māriyyah al-Qibṭiyyah ﵂ and her sister were sent by al-Muqawqis to the Prophet ﷺ as gifts. Although they struggled to imagine leaving their country, their hearts were already leaning towards Islam. Shortly after, Sayyidah Māriyyah al-Qibṭiyyah ﵂ accepted Islam and subsequently married the Prophet ﷺ.

A Joyous Arrival

When Sayyidah Māriyyah al-Qibṭiyyah ﵂ became pregnant, it brought immense joy to the Prophet ﷺ. This was a significant incident in the life of the Prophet ﷺ as none of his wives other than his first wife – Sayyidah Khadījah ﵂ – had any children from him. And by the time he married Sayyidah Māriyyah ﵂, he had lost all of his children except Sayyidah Fāṭimah ﵂. The Messenger of Allah ﷺ went through the pain of losing his children, and when Sayyidah Māriyyah ﵂ became pregnant the Prophet ﷺ honoured her by arranging for her to live on the outskirts of Medina so that she could gradually get used to life there and so that she did not have to live with the other wives. He would visit her every day and made sure that she was well taken care of. When she delivered a baby boy, they named him Ibrāhīm, as it was commanded by Allah ﷻ through Sayyidunā Jibrīl ؑ that 'you will have a boy, Ibrāhīm, the father of all the Prophets'.

The Prophet ﷺ was overjoyed with the arrival of Sayyidunā Ibrāhīm. As was the custom and tradition of the Arabs in those days, breastfeeding children used to be sent to the outskirts of the city to be breastfed by special mothers, and Ibrāhīm was sent to a foster family for this purpose. While there, the Prophet ﷺ always visited him, carrying him, kissing him affectionately, and spending time with him. His love for the baby was boundless, and the Companions recount how much he enjoyed seeing him and playing with him.

An Overwhelming Loss

When Sayyidunā Ibrāhīm was just two years old, he became sick. Almost immediately after the Prophet ﷺ went to see him and took him from Sayyidah Māriyyah رضي الله عنها, the young boy took his last breaths in the hands of the Messenger of Allah ﷻ. The Prophet ﷺ was filled with sorrow and started crying, as he endured a pain unfathomable to most – the loss of so many of his children. We all face tests and trials in our lives, but the most severely tested of all was the Prophet ﷺ. He went through the loss of all of his children except one, and when a bundle of joy illuminated his household after such a long time, he was tested with his loss as well.

It is narrated by Imam al-Bukhārī that Sayyidunā ʿAbd al-Raḥmān ibn ʿAwf رضي الله عنه looked at the Prophet ﷺ and said, 'O Messenger of Allah, you cry?' He responded and said, 'This is a mercy, ʿAbd al-Raḥmān, it is not a weakness to show your feelings. It is the mercy that Allah ﷻ put in the hearts.' The Prophet ﷺ washed and buried Ibrāhīm. Such was the beauty of the Prophet ﷺ: while his heart submitted fully to the decree of Allah ﷻ, he grieved and showed us that it is acceptable to feel sad and cry for our losses.

At the time of the death of Sayyidunā Ibrāhīm, Medina witnessed a solar eclipse, and people associated it with his death. The Prophet ﷺ dispelled such myths and said these famous words, 'Neither the Sun nor the Moon go through an eclipse because of the death of anyone. Rather, it is a sign from the signs of Allah ﷻ.'

Finding Strength in Devotion

After the death of her son, Sayyidah Māriyyah continued to stay on the outskirts of Medina, maintaining a private life and dedicating herself to worship and devotion. She did not leave the house other than for visiting the grave of Sayyidunā Ibrāhīm. Shortly after the death of Sayyidunā Ibrāhīm, the Prophet ﷺ also passed away. We can imagine the extent of her grief. In a matter of just a few days, she lost two of the most important people in her life: her son and her husband. Despite this tragedy, she found solace in the remembrance of Allah ﷻ and spent the rest of her days in privacy.

Sayyidah Māriyyah's journey in Islam, marked by her marriage to the Prophet ﷺ, left a significant impact on the relationships between the Arabs and the people of different regions, and created a strong bond between them. The Prophet ﷺ venerated her by honouring her people, and even after his passing, his instructions regarding the kind treatment of the Egyptians continued to be honoured. When Sayyidunā ʿAmr ibn al-ʿĀṣ became the governor of Egypt, he used to remember this and continued to regard his instructions.

Sayyidah Māriyyah passed away in the 16th year after the Hijrah during the rule of Sayyidunā ʿUmar, who performed the funeral prayer over her body. She was buried in al-Baqīʿ next to her son, Ibrāhīm.

The story of Sayyidah Māriyyah al-Qibṭiyyah reminds us of the diversity within the ummah and the unifying power of Islam. Her journey from Egypt to Medina, her acceptance of Islam, and her role as a bridge between cultures are profound lessons in unity and understanding. Her trials and the emotional impact of losing her son resonate as reminders of the human nature of the Prophet ﷺ and the profound wisdom embedded within life's challenges.

ZAYNAB BINT MUHAMMAD رضي الله عنها

Her early exposure to the hardships of faith and the role of being the firstborn moulded her personality into a leader and caregiver.

CHAPTER FOURTEEN

Zaynab bint Muhammad ﷺ

The Prophet ﷺ was an example of beautiful character, and he was the best among all to his family. We often wonder what it must be like to grow up in his household. How his presence must have shaped the lives of the women in his family. Loved and adored by the Prophet ﷺ and one of the women who played an essential role in shaping the Islamic community, the story of his eldest daughter Sayyidah Zaynab bint Muhammad ﷺ is inspiring.

Under the Shade of the Prophet ﷺ

Scholars collectively agree that the Prophet ﷺ had all his children – except Sayyidunā Ibrāhīm – from Sayyidah Khadījah ﷺ. He had four daughters and the eldest of them was Sayyidah Zaynab ﷺ. Her life journey began in the midst of challenges and adversities. Born in Mecca ten years before the prophethood of the Messenger of Allah ﷺ, she witnessed first-hand the trials faced by her family as they embraced Islam and navigated through the opposition of the Quraysh. Historical records give a vivid description of how the pagans and Quraysh treated the early Muslims in Mecca and how difficult their lives were. Yet, amidst all of this, Sayyidah Zaynab ﷺ was growing up under the shade of her father and the Prophet of Allah ﷺ, and her early exposure to the hardships of faith and the role of being the firstborn moulded her personality into a leader and caregiver. She helped her mother, Sayyidah Khadījah ﵂, raise her three younger sisters and also became a mentor to them.

Tested in Marriage

In the seventh year of prophethood, the Quraysh decided to boycott and outcast the Muslims in the Valley of Abū Ṭālib (Shiʿb Abī Ṭālib) for three years. They were tortured, socially boycotted, and confined to this valley with no source of food and water. The entire family of our Prophet ﷺ, Sayyidah Khadījah ﵂, and her daughters suffered in this boycott, including Sayyidah Zaynab ﵂, who braved imprisonment, starvation, and the cruelty of the disbelievers.

Her marriage to her cousin Abū al-ʿĀṣ at the age of 18 brought with it a unique set of challenges. He was the son of her aunt, that is, the sister of Sayyidah Khadījah ﵂. Sayyidah Zaynab ﵂ had two children: a daughter named Umāmah and a son named ʿAlī, who died at the age of six at the time of the conquest of Mecca. Her daughter Umāmah was a beloved granddaughter to the Prophet ﷺ, who loved her dearly. A long and arduous journey began for Sayyidah Zaynab ﵂ when her husband refused to become a Muslim (this was prior to the ruling that a Muslim cannot marry a non-Muslim). He was a very nice man and took good care of her, but his rejection of Islam put their relationship under great strain. She was the daughter of the Prophet ﷺ, and she believed in him wholeheartedly. How painful it must have been for her to have her husband, whom she loved so much, reject the truth.

The time for migration came, and the Prophet ☙ migrated to Medina with his family, but Sayyidah Zaynab ☙ stayed back. When the Battle of Badr took place, her husband fought against the Muslims and was captured. It was a custom at the time that those captured in war could be freed if their family gave a ransom in exchange. The Prophet ☙ announced the same ruling in Medina for the prisoners of Mecca. When Sayyidah Zaynab ☙ came to know about this, she sent a necklace as ransom to free her husband. It was the same necklace that her mother, Sayyidah Khadījah ☙, had gifted her as her wedding gift. It held such sentimental value for the Prophet ☙ that when he saw it, he began to cry. His heart melted as her memories came back, and he requested the Companions to give him approval to release the prisoner without the ransom. He said, 'I will set him free without money, but he must promise that he will send Zaynab back to Medina.' Abū al-ʿĀṣ kept his promise and sent Sayyidah Zaynab ☙ to Medina once he reached Mecca.

A Happy Reunion

The difficult period of waiting and hoping began for Sayyidah Zaynab ☙ as she stayed in Medina with her two children while her husband lived in Mecca as a non-Muslim. Things took a turn when he went out with a caravan on a trade trip, and the Muslims attacked the caravan. Abū al-ʿĀṣ ran away to Medina, looking for Sayyidah Zaynab ☙, and when he found her, she took him under her care and announced to everyone that no one must harm him as he is in her protection. This was another interesting custom of the time, which dictated that if a person reached a Muslim land and came under the protection of a person or household, whether Muslim or non-Muslim, they could not be harmed. When the Prophet ﷺ heard his daughter's voice, he was shocked. The courage that Sayyidah Zaynab showed in those moments was exemplary. She did not lose hope in Allah ﷻ and continued her efforts to try and convince her husband of the truth of Islam. Eventually, her efforts paid off and Abū al-ʿĀṣ finally accepted Islam. Once he became a Muslim, the Prophet ﷺ re-married them. Her courage and continuous efforts did not go to waste. The unique strength she inherited from her parents was evident in the way she endured trial after trial without giving up.

A Legacy of Courage and Compassion

Unfortunately, Sayyidah Zaynab's reunion with her husband was short-lived. She passed away shortly after as a result of the severe injuries she sustained during her migration from Mecca to Medina. Her final moments were spent in the love and care of the Prophet ﷺ, who personally laid her to rest in her grave and prayed over her. He said, 'I was very worried and disturbed by the weak physique of Zaynab and I prayed that Allah ﷻ relieve her from the squeeze of the grave.' She was his first child, whom he raised and loved.

Sayyidah Zaynab's story embodies the essence of courage and grace. Her endurance and legacy serve as an inspiration for all believers, emphasising the significance of maintaining steadfastness in the face of challenges and holding fast to the values of compassion, unity, and love for the sake of Allah.

CHAPTER FIFTEEN

Ruqayyah bint Muhammad ﵂

As we explore the lives of the blessed women of the Prophet's household, we come across the inspiring story of his second daughter, Sayyidah Ruqayyah ﵂. Even though little is known about her, her contribution to the building of an Islamic nation cannot be overlooked.

A Blessing in Disguise

Ruqayyah bint Muhammad ibn ʿAbdullāh was the only daughter of the Prophet ﷺ who migrated twice, once to Abyssinia and then from Abyssinia to Medina. She was tested significantly throughout her life, and just like the other women who believed in the message of Islam, remained courageous and steadfast.

Her first test came in the form of her marriage. Both Sayyidah Ruqayyah ﵂ and her sister, Sayyidah Umm Kulthūm ﵂, were married to the sons of Abū Lahab. When Allah ﷻ revealed Sūrah al-Masad, which commences with, 'May the hands of Abū Lahab perish, as well as he himself', Abū Lahab and his wife were infuriated. They pushed their sons to divorce both daughters of the

Prophet ﷺ. Distraught, Sayyidah Ruqayyah and Umm Kulthūm ﷺ came back to their father's house. However, we know that when Allah ﷻ gives us a great test and we hold onto Him with hope, He replaces our loss with something better.

The Prophet ﷺ said:

مَن ترك شيئًا لله عوَّضه الله خيرًا منه

'Whenever a servant of Allah leaves something for Allah, Allah will replace it with something better.'

(Musnad Aḥmad)

And true to His promise, Allah ﷻ replaced Sayyidah Ruqayyah's loss with something much better: marriage to the noble Companion Sayyidunā 'Uthmān ibn 'Affān ؓ. After their marriage, they migrated to Abyssinia for a short while before hearing of an improved situation for the Muslims in Mecca. Under the pretence that torture and persecution had lessened and things were easier for the Muslims, they decided to go back to Mecca. After a long and arduous journey, they discovered that what they had heard was not true and so they were forced to return back to Abyssinia immediately.

Victory and Loss

While in Abyssinia, Sayyidah Ruqayyah ؓ delivered a son named 'Abdullāh, who died after developing severe eye injuries. It was a tragic loss that severely grieved her, and Sayyidah Ruqayyah ؓ died shortly after, just two years after the Hijrah. While the Prophet ﷺ was fighting in Badr, she fell ill, and when he received news of her illness, he ordered Sayyidunā ʿUthmān to leave the battlefield and be with her. The Prophet could not go to see her or pray on her, as the call of Allah was superior. As the Muslims emerged victorious in the Battle of Badr, Sayyidah Ruqayyah passed away and was buried in al-Baqīʿ in Medina.

Her death, just as her life, was remarkable as it left a mark on the lives of the Prophet and a major Companion, namely Sayyidunā ʿUthmān. Although her life was relatively short and her presence in recorded history may be limited, Sayyidah Ruqayyah's experiences highlight the themes of faith, sacrifice, and perseverance. Her story serves as a reminder that the trials and difficulties faced by the believers, even during moments of personal grief, are opportunities for spiritual growth and closeness to Allah.

CHAPTER SIXTEEN

Umm Kulthūm bint Muhammad ﵂

Episodes of loss and pain teach us many lessons. They can either break us and take us away from faith or make us stronger and help us rely on Allah ﷻ with even more conviction and strength than before. Sayyidah Umm Kulthūm ﵂, the daughter of the Prophet ﷺ, is a testament to these qualities. Her story exhibits faith and resilience and is a source of inspiration for all believers.

An Image of Her Mother

Sayyidah Umm Kulthūm ﵂ was the third daughter of the Prophet ﷺ and Sayyidah Khadījah ﵂. Her full name was Umm Kulthūm bint Muhammad ibn ʿAbdullāh, and she was the second wife of Sayyidunā ʿUthmān ibn ʿAffān ﵁ after her elder sister, Sayyidah Ruqayyah ﵂, passed away. From a young age, she was exceptionally responsible as she was born before prophethood and saw the hardships of the early years in Mecca. She took care of her mother in her sickness and later migrated to Medina with her little sister Sayyidah Fāṭimah ﵂, her brother-in-law Sayyidunā ʿAlī ﵁, and her stepmother Sayyidah Sawdah ﵂.

The passing of her mother affected her profoundly and caused her great sorrow. She was the only grown up daughter to stay with the Prophet ﷺ after the death of Sayyidah Khadījah, as Sayyidah Zaynab was married at the time and Sayyidah Ruqayyah was already in Abyssinia. In the absence of the elder sisters, she assumed the role of the caregiver in the household of the Prophet ﷺ. She was the one who comforted her father and took care of her younger sister, Sayyidah Fāṭimah, all the while mourning the loss of her dear mother. She was a reflection of her mother's selflessness, as even when her own sense of loss was profound, she focused on the care and needs of her father and sister. This was the generous spirit that marked the character of every woman in the household of the Prophet ﷺ, and she was no different.

A New Beginning

Similar to the case of her elder sister Sayyidah Ruqayyah, she was also married to one of the sons of Abū Lahab, ʿUtaybah, but the marriage was not consummated. When the verses in Sūrah al-Masad were revealed, reading 'May the hands of Abū Lahab perish', Abū Lahab ordered both his sons to divorce the daughters to hurt the Prophet ﷺ. Soon after that, she migrated to Medina with Sayyidah Fāṭimah and Sayyidah Sawdah and Sayyidunā ʿAlī.

ʿUtaybah was a wicked man who was rude and unpleasant to the Prophet ﷺ. After the divorce, he attacked and humiliated the Prophet ﷺ, prompting him to make a duʿā' against him. He said, 'May Allah ﷻ unleash his dog upon you.' And sure enough, the duʿā' of the Prophet ﷺ was answered. Not long after, he was traveling to Syria on a trade journey, and in the land of Jordan, he was attacked and devoured by a lion. In this, we take lesson and reassurance that the du'ā' of someone who has faced injustice reaches Allah ﷻ without any barriers.

Once Sayyidah Umm Kulthūm رضي الله عنها migrated to Medina, she remarried for the second time. Since Sayyidah Ruqayyah رضي الله عنها had passed away, Sayyidunā 'Uthmān ibn 'Affān رضي الله عنه was overcome with grief, and the biggest reason for his grief was that his connection with the Prophet ﷺ was broken after her death. When the Prophet ﷺ came to know about this, he offered him the hand of his other daughter, Sayyidah Umm Kulthūm رضي الله عنها. Thus, her second marriage was to a noble and pious man, namely Sayyidunā 'Uthmān ibn 'Affān رضي الله عنه. He was a blessed man in so many ways, but perhaps the biggest blessing in his life was the honour of being married to two of the daughters of the Prophet ﷺ. It was this honour that earned him the title of Dhū al-Nūrayn (the Owner of Two Lights). The marriage was decreed by Allah ﷻ and was then ultimately revealed to the Prophet ﷺ. The wedding took place in the month of Rabī' al-Awwal, and she left her house to be with him in Jumādā al-Thānī.

The Prophet ﷺ could not have been happier, as he greatly loved and admired Sayyidunā 'Uthmān رضي الله عنه. His contributions to Islam were great, and there was no one better than him for his noble daughter. It was Sayyidunā 'Uthmān رضي الله عنه who came forward for the Jaysh al-'Usrah (Army of Need), donating all of his supplies generously for the sake of Allah ﷻ. The Prophet ﷺ said, 'Nothing shall harm 'Uthmān after what he just did today.' When he was giving his daughter to Sayyidunā 'Uthmān رضي الله عنه in marriage, the Prophet ﷺ said to her, 'Truly your husband is the closest in resemblance to your forefather Ibrāhīm and your father Muhammad.'

Despite being the wife of Sayyidunā ʿUthmān and the daughter of the Prophet, Sayyidah Umm Kulthūm did not have children of her own. This serves as a reminder to us that the blessings of Allah come in various forms. It is His decision and His distribution alone, and His decrees are full of wisdom.

An Early Departure

Sayyidah Umm Kulthūm exhibited courage and perseverance throughout her life, leaving behind a legacy of love and compassion for her family and for the future generations. She died at the very young age of 28, passing away in the month of Shaʿbān, nine years after the Hijrah. The Prophet grieved her loss and remembered her noble character as he put her in the grave and prayed over her body.

FĀṬIMAH BINT MUHAMMAD ﵂

*The Prophet ﷺ said,
'The best women among
the people of Paradise are
Khadījah bint Khuwaylid,
Fāṭimah bint Muhammad,
Maryam bint 'Imrān, and
Asiyah bint Muzāḥim -
the wife of Pharaoh.'*

CHAPTER SEVENTEEN

Fāṭimah bint Muhammad ﷺ

Among the four daughters of the Prophet ﷺ, the one who is most well-known and who has the highest status in Islam is the leader of the women in Jannah, Sayyidah Fāṭimah bint Muhammad ﷺ. Her life is rich with lessons, and her character is a beacon of guidance for Muslims around the world.

The Shining One

Fāṭimah bint Muhammad ibn 'Abdullāh ﷺ had a beautiful nick-name, namely Fāṭimah al-Zahrā' (The Shining One). The beauty and radiance of her name was reflected in her character. She was well-known for being patient and demonstrating forbearance, but her most defining characteristic was how she acted with excellence in every situation. She was the only child of the Prophet ﷺ whose offspring survived, and this is why she was known as the link of al-Muṣṭafā (The Chosen One), who is none other than the Messenger of Allah ﷺ. She was also lovingly called Umm Abīhā (The Mother of her Father) because she resembled the Prophet ﷺ strikingly and took care of him after the death of her mother, Sayyidah Khadījah ﷺ.

She was the fourth and youngest daughter of the Prophet ﷺ and Sayyidah Khadījah ؓ, born four years before prophethood. Growing up as a Muslim from early childhood, she witnessed the torment and persecution that her father, mother, and the early believers faced, which undoubtedly played a significant role in shaping her strong character and unwavering faith. Sayyidah Fāṭimah ؓ was quite young when her mother Sayyidah Khadījah ؓ died; after this tragedy, her elder sister Umm Kulthūm ؓ took care of her, along with their stepmother, Sayyidah Sawdah ؓ. She migrated to Medina with her sister, step mother, and Sayyidunā ʿAlī ؓ.

She was known as the best woman of her era and is one of the best women of Jannah. She narrated several Hadiths from the Prophet ﷺ, and the Companions also narrated many Hadiths from her.

A Special Status

Sayyidunā ʿAbdullāh ibn ʿAbbās ؓ reported in a Hadith recorded by Imam Aḥmad that the Prophet ﷺ said, 'The best women among the people of Paradise are Khadījah bint Khuwaylid, Fāṭimah bint Muhammad, Maryam bint ʿImrān, and Āsiyah bint Muzāḥim – the wife of Pharaoh.' These were the four best women of Paradise, all of whom led remarkable lives of piety, steadfastness, and stellar character: Khadījah bint Khuwaylid (the first wife of the Prophet ﷺ), Fāṭimah bint Muhammad (his daughter), Maryam bint ʿImrān (the mother of Prophet ʿĪsā ؑ), and Āsiyah (the wife of Pharaoh).

The Prophet ﷺ adored her and she was the coolness of his eyes. It was the Sunnah of the Prophet ﷺ to go to the mosque immediately upon returning from every trip and battle. After this, he would make sure to visit Sayyidah Fāṭimah ﵂ and see her before going to his wives. She had a special status with the Prophet of Allah ﷺ and he was extremely protective of her. In a narration from al-Bukhārī, the Prophet ﷺ was reported to have said, 'Fāṭimah is a part of me, and he who makes her angry makes me angry.'

When Sayyidah 'Ā'ishah ﵂ was asked who the most beloved person to the Prophet ﷺ was, she responded, 'Fāṭimah.' She was also asked who the most beloved from among the men was, and she responded, 'Her husband 'Alī.' She was also reported to have said, 'I have not seen anyone who resembled the Prophet ﷺ in speech the way she [Fāṭimah] does.' Whenever Sayyidah Fāṭimah ﵂ would visit the Prophet ﷺ and enter into a room where he was present, he would stand up to greet her, kiss her, and welcome her. She would do the same for him when he came to visit her in her house.

She had a special place in the heart of the Prophet ﷺ, who would never say no to her for anything and detested seeing her unhappy. Sayyidah Fāṭimah ﵂ once came to the Prophet ﷺ and told him that people say that you get upset when your daughter gets upset, yet 'Alī is planning to marry the daughter of Abū Jahl. The Prophet ﷺ was not happy to hear this. He stood up, and after reading the declaration of faith, said, 'I have given my daughter to Abū al-'Āṣ ibn al-Rabī' and he treated her very well, and Fāṭimah bint Muhammad is part of me. I do not like her to be tested, and by Allah, she cannot be together in the same house with the daughter of an enemy of Allah.' So Sayyidunā 'Alī ؓ abandoned the idea of marrying the daughter of Abū Jahl. He did not marry anyone else as long as he was married to Sayyidah Fāṭimah ؓ.

The special status of Sayyidah Fāṭimah ؓ is evident from a Hadith in which the Prophet ﷺ said, 'An angel came to me today that had never descended to the Earth and he sought permission from his Lord Allah to greet me with peace and to give me the glad tidings that Fāṭimah is the best of the women of Paradise and that al-Ḥasan and al-Ḥusayn are the best of the youth of the people of Paradise.'

A Kind Heart and Grateful Nature

Sayyidah Fāṭimah ؓ was deeply affected by the injustice done to her father, and even though she did not have the power to stand up against it, she would do whatever she could to comfort and relieve him. An incident from the early days of Islam stands out as a moving example of her love for the Prophet ﷺ. While the Prophet ﷺ was praying in the courtyard of the Ka'bah, some of the disbelievers came and threw the intestine of a camel on him. The Prophet ﷺ could not get up from the state of prostration due to its weight. When Fāṭimah saw this, she ran to him crying and removed the load from his back, saying, 'Oh my father!' She cleaned the dirt and impurity from him and invocated against those who did this to her father.

Sayyidah Fāṭimah ؓ was the beloved daughter of the Messenger of Allah ﷻ and the wife of one of the greatest Companions, who would go on to become the fourth Caliph of the Islamic nation. Yet, throughout her time on this Earth she lived a humble life without luxury. In comparison to our modern needs and luxuries, her home was basic and minimal. She was married to her cousin, Sayyidunā ʿAlī ؓ, who was very close to the Prophet ﷺ. For their marriage, the Prophet ﷺ arranged the basic necessities of their home, such as leather, a water pitcher, a wooden bed, and some cushions. Despite such limited comforts, their home was filled with laughter and happiness.

Sayyidah Fāṭimah ؓ used to work very hard, as she did not receive any help to divide the work at home. It is mentioned in a Hadith that once she came to the Prophet ﷺ and requested for a helper. This was at a time in Medina when wealth was coming to the Muslims. The Prophet ﷺ was not unaware of her struggles, nor was he indifferent to her hardships. She was a piece of his heart and one of the best women of her time, yet he excused himself from giving her material help. What he gave her was even better – an invitation to the remembrance of Allah ﷻ. He told her that it would suffice her and give her more energy than having a helper share the workload. After each obligatory ṣalāh and before going to bed, he advised her to say:

تُسَبِّحِينَ اللَّهَ عِنْدَ مَنَامِكِ ثَلاَثًا وَثَلاَثِينَ، وَتَحْمَدِينَ اللَّهَ ثَلاَثًا وَثَلاَثِينَ، وَتُكَبِّرِينَ اللَّهَ
أَرْبَعًا وَثَلاَثِينَ

'When you go to sleep, say subḥānallāh (glory be to Allah) 33 times, alḥamdulillāh (all praise is due to Allah) 33 times, and Allāhu akbar (Allah is great) 34 times.'

(al-Bukhārī , 5361)

Following the Prophet ﷺ

Sayyidah Fāṭimah's whole life was marked by incredible moments, but perhaps the most memorable of them was at the time of the death of the Prophet ﷺ. She was his only child that survived. She was his reflection, his admiration, and she loved him as much as he loved her. While the Prophet ﷺ was in his final moments, she was next to him, crying. He asked her to come closer and whispered something in her ears. She started crying even harder. He then said something else, and she began smiling. She did not tell anyone what he said to her in those moments until much later.

Sayyidah ʿĀ'ishah ؓ later asked her what the Prophet ﷺ had told her that had made her cry, and she replied, 'The first thing he said to me which made me cry harder was that he did not have much time left before he would go back to Allah ﷻ. That is when I started crying very hard. Then he whispered again and said that I will be the first one to follow him after his death. And I smiled.'

When the Prophet ﷺ had passed away and they had buried him, Sayyidah Fāṭimah was inconsolable. She was so full of grief that she said to them, 'How could you get yourselves to throw dust over him?' They replied that this was what he had taught them, and even though they were devastated themselves, it was something they had to do.

Sayyidah Fāṭimah ؓ died just six months after the death of the Prophet ﷺ at the young age of 28. She was buried by Sayyidunā ʿAlī ؓ in al-Baqīʿ, and he prayed over her. Sayyidah Fāṭimah's life is an embodiment of devotion, strength, humility, and love.

Her relationship with the Prophet ﷺ, her marriage to Sayyidunā ʿAlī ﷺ and her role as a mother exemplify the qualities that every believer should aspire to cultivate. Her legacy continues to inspire generations of Muslims to seek closeness to Allah ﷻ through acts of kindness, patience, and unwavering faith.

PART TWO

Female Companions

ASMĀ’ BINT ABĪ BAKR ﵂

Her commitment to serving the Prophet ﷺ and her father and providing them comfort is beautifully depicted by her nickname - The Woman of the Two Belts.

CHAPTER ONE

Asmā' bint Abī Bakr رضي الله عنها

When the light of Islam illuminated the household of the Prophet ﷺ, it spread around to those who had faith in his honesty and integrity. Among those who believed were noble women who not only accepted his message but also left their own mark on the history of Islam. One such woman was the daughter of Sayyidunā Abū Bakr ﷺ, Asmā' bint Abī Bakr ﷺ. The story of Sayyidah Asmā' ﷺ is a remarkable one, as she played a pivotal role in the early days of Islam.

A Courageous Stance

Sayyidah Asmā' ﷺ was the older half-sister of the Prophet's wife, Sayyidah 'Ā'ishah ﷺ. Her mother was called Qutaylah, and she was not a Muslim. Sayyidah Asmā' ﷺ was one of the early Muslims. In fact, she was the 18th person to accept Islam in Mecca and spent a lot of time in the house of the Prophet ﷺ, learning from him directly. She was married to Sayyidunā Zubayr ibn al-'Awwām ﷺ, who was a relative of the Prophet ﷺ from his paternal side, and was also one of the ten people who were given the glad tidings of Jannah.

Sayyidah Asmā’ ﵂ was a woman of great courage. Her firm standing at the time of the migration of the Prophet ﷺ and Sayyidunā Abū Bakr ﵁ to Medina demonstrates her strength and self-confidence. She was a woman of conviction, and this was evident from the way she held her ground in front of the persecutors. When Allah ﷻ gave permission to the Prophet ﷺ to migrate to Medina, he chose Sayyidunā Abū Bakr ﵁ to go along with him on the journey. After they had departed, Sayyidah Asmā’ ﵂ stayed in the house of her father. Soon after, a group of men from the Quraysh, led by Abū Jahl, came knocking on the door. They demanded to know where her father was, but she insisted that she did not know. Abū Jahl was so furious that he slapped her across the face. It is reported that he slapped her so hard that the earrings she was wearing fell off. Sayyidah Asmā’ ﵂ remained strong in the face of these tyrants, and her powerful stance is remembered as an inspiration to this day.

A Joyous Occasion in Medina

Sayyidah Asmā’ ﵂ was pregnant when she followed her father and the Prophet ﷺ in the migration path, where she was accompanied with her stepmother Umm Rūmān ﵂ and her younger stepsister Sayyidah ‘Ā’ishah ﵂. As soon as they reached Medina, Asmā’ gave birth to her son, ‘Abdullāh ibn al-Zubayr. It was a joyous occasion for the Muslims in Medina as he was the first newborn baby in Medina and was named by the Prophet ﷺ himself, who carried him and performed the Sunnah of rubbing the palate of the newborn baby with honey or dates – a ritual known as al-taḥnīk. The Prophet ﷺ took a date, chewed it to soften it, and then rubbed the softened paste on the palate of the baby.

When we discuss and analyse the migration to Medina, the name of Sayyidah Asmā' ؓ is among the first ones that come to mind, as she played a central role in its success. As the Prophet ﷺ and Sayyidunā Abū Bakr ؓ concealed themselves for three nights in the cave of Thawr (which is situated three miles from Mecca), Sayyidah Asmā' ؓ would come every day from her house with food and water. Heavily pregnant, Asmā' displayed dedication, loyalty, and courage, still mustering the strength to carry heavy goods to sustain her father and the Prophet ﷺ. She is famously remembered for an incident that beautifully encapsulates these characteristics. Unable to put both the food and water on a camel, Sayyidah Asmā' ؓ took her belt and tore it in half, using both belts to tie the goods. Her commitment to serving the Prophet ﷺ and her father and providing them comfort is beautifully depicted by her nickname Dhāt al-Niṭāqayn – The Woman of the Two Belts.

Nurturing a Righteous Son

The life of Sayyidah Asmā' in Medina – alongside her husband Zubayr ibn al-'Awwām and their son 'Abdullāh ibn al-Zubayr – was one of poverty, but her family was blessed with the closeness of the Prophet ﷺ. She used to send her son to the house of his aunt, Sayyidah 'Ā'ishah ؓ, to learn first-hand from the Prophet of Allah ﷺ. He would spend so much time with Sayyidah 'Ā'ishah ؓ that even though she did not have a son, she was given the moniker Umm 'Abdullāh, which translates to the mother of 'Abdullāh. 'Abdullāh ibn al-Zubayr ؓ grew up to be a famous Companion and narrated many Hadiths of the Prophet ﷺ.

Sayyidah Asmā' ؓ grew even more courageous as time passed, gaining from the strength of her faith. Sayyidunā 'Abdullāh ibn al-Zubayr ؓ was encouraged to become the Caliph at the time of Yazīd ibn Mu'āwiyah by the inhabitants of many major regions, including Syria, Iraq, Mecca, and Medina. As he led an army to take over the caliphate from the Umayyad dynasty, al-Ḥajjāj ibn Yūsuf al-Thaqafī, who lived in Baghdad, led an army and started fighting against 'Abdullāh ibn al-Zubayr ؓ. Many of the supporters of 'Abdullāh ibn al-Zubayr ؓ deserted him, and his sphere of influence was reduced to the sacred city of Mecca. He came to his mother for advice and said to her, 'O my mother, should I surrender to al-Ḥajjāj or continue to fight? They promised me that if I surrender, I will live, and if I continue to fight, the possibility of my death is almost certain.'

Sayyidah Asmā' ؓ was a very old woman at this time, and was reported to have been over 100 years of age. She was witnessing her only son fighting and was now given the opportunity to see his agony end. She looked at him and said, 'Did you fight for the truth or for falsehood?' He replied, 'For the truth.' She said, 'Then continue fighting.' 'Abdullāh ibn al-Zubayr ؓ died in battle shortly thereafter. Al-Ḥajjāj asked Asmā' to come and take his body, but she refused to comply with the oppressor and instead displayed outstanding courage and belief in the Judgment of Allah ﷻ by responding, 'You took from him his life in this world, but he took your Hereafter.'

A Legacy of Courage and Sacrifice

Asmā' bint Abī Bakr died in Mecca a few days after burying her son. Her life teaches us the importance of standing up for what is right, even in the face of daunting challenges. Her sacrifices, courage, and unyielding faith provide a timeless example of a Muslim woman's dedication to her family, community, and religion. Her legacy continues to inspire believers to remain steadfast and principled in their pursuit of truth and justice.

CHAPTER TWO

Umm Sulaym bint Milḥān رضي الله عنها

There were people in the history of Islam who prioritised their religion and belief above all else, refusing to compromise in the face of adversities. One such personality was al-Rumayṣā' bint Milḥān or Umm Sulaym ﷺ, a Companion of the Prophet ﷺ, the mother of a prominent Companion who narrated many Hadiths, and one of the five women who pledged their allegiance to the Prophet ﷺ in Bayt al-Riḍwān.

A Defender of Faith

The story of Sayyidah Umm Sulaym ﷺ is a story of love and devotion towards Allah ﷻ, His Messenger ﷺ, and the message of Islam. Even before she accepted Islam, Sayyidah Umm Sulaym was well-known for her exceptional character, independence in attitude and mind, and strong intellect. She holds a distinguished place among the prominent female Companions of the Prophet ﷺ, having learnt from him and leaving behind a mark of her own.

Sayyidah Umm Sulaym ﷺ came from Medina, where she lived with her husband, Mālik, and son, Sayyidunā Anas ibn Mālik ﷺ,

a famous Companion of the Prophet ﷺ. She embraced Islam while her husband was on a trip to Syria, and when he returned to discover her decision, he was unhappy and rejected her invitations to the truth. Despite this, she continued to stay with him and decided to dedicate her time and focus on their son, Sayyidunā Anas ibn Mālik رضي الله عنه, teaching him the basics of Islamic belief. Sayyidah Umm Sulaym رضي الله عنها would sit with her son and teach him the shahādah, the declaration of the Oneness of Allah ﷻ. Upon hearing this, her husband became angry and tried to encourage her to stop, beseeching her to 'not ruin his religion'. But Sayyidah Umm Sulaym رضي الله عنها would respond, 'I am not ruining his religion, rather this is the true religion.' She exerted the utmost degree of efforts to engrain this simple truth into the mind of her young child and encouraged him to repeat the declaration of faith emphatically. Sayyidunā Anas ibn Mālik رضي الله عنه went on to become one of the most trusted Companions of the Prophet ﷺ, and she played a crucial role in his upbringing as a strong believer.

Sayyidah Umm Sulaym رضي الله عنها was struck with a tragedy when her husband, who did not want to accept Islam and decided to leave his wife and child, died on the way to Syria. Left a widow and single mother at a young age, Sayyidah Umm Sulaym رضي الله عنها directed all of her focus and time to the upbringing of her son. She was devoted to his care to the point that she would say, 'I will not wean Anas until he leaves my breast, and I will not marry until Anas orders me to'.

Islam as a Dowry

Sayyidah Umm Sulaym ﵂ was soon offered a marriage proposal by a man named Zayd ibn Sahl or, as he is more famously known, Abū Ṭalḥah ﵁. Even though he was a man of wealth and honour and was eager to marry her, Sayyidah Umm Sulaym ﵂ did not accept his proposal because he was a disbeliever, and instead laid down a condition of marriage – his acceptance of Islam. In pursuit of this, she made efforts to highlight the futile nature of their worship of false gods and said words to him that would shake his conscience. She said, 'O Abū Ṭalḥah, you are an intelligent man. Yet you worship a tree that is carved by a man from the Banū al-Najjār tribe, and should it be touched by fire, it would burn! Do you not feel ashamed that you worship a tree? By Allah, I do want to marry you, for you are a man of honour and station. But if you accept Islam, I will seek no dowry from you, and I will want nothing more.'

Sayyidah Umm Sulaym ﵂ was intent on her decision and stayed true to it despite Sayyidunā Abū Ṭalḥah's many attempts to persuade her otherwise. Every time he approached her with the intention of marriage, she would respond to him by saying, 'My dowry is that you proclaim that there is no God but Allah, and Muhammad is the Messenger of Allah.' She was a young widow with a small child to care for and had no resources, yet her priority was her faith, and she made no compromise on it.

Eventually, he started seeing the truth as Allah ﷻ opened his heart to Islam, and he became a Muslim. When they finally got married, the Muslims would say about her dowry (mahr): 'We have never heard of a mahr that was more valuable and precious than that of Umm Sulaym, for she made Islam her mahr.' Hence forth, she was called by the nickname 'The Lady of the Great Dowry'.

A Shining Example of Wisdom and Patience

Sayyidah Umm Sulaym was described as a woman of profound wisdom and patience. Her life was marked by struggles that strengthened her faith in Allah and gave her the power of resilience. One of the most famous stories with regard to her wisdom and patience occurred after her marriage to Sayyidunā Abū Ṭalḥah, when she gave birth to a son named 'Umar. The child was constantly ill, and while Sayyidunā Abū Ṭalḥah was once on a trip, he passed away. When Sayyidunā Abū Ṭalḥah returned, she did not want to inform him of their loss immediately, as he would be full of grief. Instead, she beautified herself for him and had intercourse with him, before giving him the sad news. The way that Sayyidah Umm Sulaym broke the news to her husband is also exemplary. She said to him, 'If a tribe gave a tribe something to keep with them for a while, and after a while the first tribe asked for it back, what would you say?' He responded, 'It is theirs, so they can take it back.' She said, 'Seek your reward from Allah as He took back what was His.' Upon hearing this, Sayyidunā Abū Ṭalḥah was devastated, but Allah blessed them with another child that very night. Sayyidah Umm Sulaym eventually gave birth to a baby boy named 'Abdullāh ibn Abī Talhah, who went on to become a great Companion.

Sayyidah Umm Sulaym showed great courage, wisdom, and faith in Allah by refraining from complaining about her loss and showing empathy towards her husband. She did not panic or lose sight of the greater vision of life.

Serving the Prophet ﷺ

Sayyidah Umm Sulaym had an exemplary marriage with her husband. Their household was one that was devoted to the Prophet ﷺ and the service of Muslims and Islam. The Prophet ﷺ used to visit their home, and she would provide him with a mat to pray on. He would also sometimes take an afternoon nap in their house, and as he slept, she would take the perspiration from his forehead and collect it. On one occasion, when the Prophet ﷺ woke up from his nap, he asked: 'Umm Sulaym, what are you doing?' She replied, 'I am taking these [drops of perspiration] as a means of barakah (blessing) from you.'

Sayyidunā Anas ibn Mālik narrated another incident that shows the extent of his mother's love for the Prophet ﷺ. On one occasion, the Prophet ﷺ entered the house of Sayyidunā Anas ibn Mālik while his mother was present. He saw a leather bag that contained water and drank from it until all of it was finished. At this moment, Sayyidah Umm Sulaym did something fascinating that demonstrates to us just how highly the Companions of the Prophet ﷺ revered the Prophet ﷺ and sought his blessings. She took the leather bag, cut off the part of it from where he drank, and kept it as a source of blessing.

Sayyidah Umm Sulaym also sent her son Anas ibn Mālik to stay with the Prophet Muhammad ﷺ for ten years to both serve him and learn sacred knowledge from him. Because of his proximity to the Prophet ﷺ, he went on to narrate numerous Hadiths and became one of the most prominent Companions. It was the vision of Sayyidah Umm Sulaym for him that allowed him to reach this position, as she understood that staying under the shade of the Prophet ﷺ would teach him the most valuable lessons in life.

Sayyidunā Anas ibn Mālik ﷺ described how his mother prioritised his upbringing and exerted all efforts to ensure he became a strong believer. He narrates a time when his mother brought him to the Prophet ﷺ and asked him to pray for Anas. The Prophet ﷺ prayed for him three times and invoked blessings for him. In another profound narration, he says, 'I have seen the result of two in this world regarding wealth and progeny, and regarding the third du'ā', I hope to see it answered in the Hereafter.' By this statement, Anas meant that he had seen the result of two supplications made by the Prophet ﷺ for him: righteous knowledge and many children.

Brave and Knowledgeable

Sayyidah Umm Sulaym ﷺ was a woman of courage who did not bow down to fear. It is said that on the day of the Battle of Ḥunayn, which took place after the Conquest of Mecca, she went out with the Muslims holding a dagger that she possessed. When her husband Sayyidunā Abū Ṭalḥah ﷺ saw her, he informed the Prophet ﷺ and told him, 'Look at what she has with her.' The Prophet ﷺ smiled because he knew that she was a woman of courage and wisdom. He asked her what she intended to do with the dagger, and she replied to him that if any non-believer came close to her, she would kill him. She said to the Prophet ﷺ, 'O Messenger of Allah, kill all those people who do not believe in Allah ﷻ or who believed because we conquered Mecca.' To this, the Prophet ﷺ responded, 'Allah is more than enough for us, and He has showered us with excellence', thereby explaining that he did not need to kill these people to establish the truth. Her extreme love for Allah and loyalty to the Prophet are evident from this courageous act, demonstrating how she did not hesitate at the prospect of fighting in battle.

Sayyidah Umm Sulaym was also a woman of great knowledge and intellect. Her deep insight is evident from an incident in which she clarified important information regarding women during the Hajj ceremony. Sayyidunā ʿAbdullāh ibn ʿAbbās, who was a famous Companion of the Prophet, was in Hajj with a group of people from Medina. The people asked him about a woman who got her menses after performing ṭawāf al-ifāḍah. They wanted to know if she could leave Mecca or stay until Hajj ended. Sayyidunā ʿAbdullāh ibn ʿAbbās told them that they could leave, but he insisted that once they reach Medina, they should confirm the correctness of the answer from someone knowledgeable, and he specifically named Sayyidah Umm Sulaym as being a specialist in this matter. She confirmed that the opinion he presented was correct, as she had heard it herself from Sayyidah Ṣafiyyah, the wife of the Prophet.

Sayyidah Umm Sulaym was keen on learning and gaining knowledge about sensitive matters of religion and did not shy away from asking questions. She once asked a question that stirred both awe and discomfort: 'What should a woman do if her dream mirrors that of a man, ultimately leading to ritual impurity?' Sayyidah ʿĀ'ishah, who had a wealth of knowledge herself and was present with the Prophet at the time felt uncomfortable and said that this type of question is humiliating for women. But the Prophet, in his wisdom and kindness, addressed Sayyidah Umm Sulaym and answered the question. He told her that if a woman experiences this, she should take the ritual bath the same way as a man who experiences this.

Lasting Influence

Sayyidah Umm Sulaym ﵂ was a woman of virtue and high status in the Islamic community. Her dedication to the righteous upbringing of her son and her courageous defence of the Muslims earned her the honour of being one of the women of Paradise.

Jābir ibn ʿAbdullāh ﵄ narrated:

'The Prophet ﷺ said, "I saw myself (in a dream) entering Paradise and behold! I saw al-Rumayṣā', Abū Ṭalḥah's wife."'

(al-Bukhārī)

Sayyidah Umm Sulaym's biggest legacy was her spirit of serving the Prophet ﷺ. She was content with little and did not have much to herself. When she sent her beloved son, Sayyidunā Anas ibn Mālik ﵁, to serve the Prophet ﷺ, she said to him, 'O Messenger of Allah, people give you gifts and I am giving you my son as a gift. Let him serve you and learn from you.' It was her deep wisdom and foresight that gave way to a legacy of knowledge and servitude and kept her name alive for generations to come. She was a woman of purity, integrity, and great morals and became a source of immense goodness for her community.

She passed away at the young age of 40 during the caliphate of Muʿāwiyah ﵁. Sayyidah Umm Sulaym's story serves as a poignant reminder for all seekers of knowledge and for those who dedicate their lives in the service of Allah ﷻ. It reminds us that a life – though brief – can shine brilliantly, guiding others through the labyrinth of faith, knowledge, and unwavering commitment to the divine path.

CHAPTER THREE

Al-Farīʿah bint Mālik ﷺ

Some of the prominent women at the time of the Prophet ﷺ are often not remembered by their names but by the impact they had on the history of Islam. They left valuable lessons for generations to come, and these lessons became a part of their legacy. One of these prominent women was al-Farīʿah bint Mālik ﷺ, an example of honesty and devotion.

A Noble Lineage

Sayyidah al-Farīʿah bint Mālik ﷺ was a woman of remarkable lineage and came from an honourable family of warriors, leaders, and scholars. Her father was the esteemed Companion Mālik ibn Sinān ibn ʿUbayd al-Anṣārī al-Khudrī ﷺ, who was a significant figure in Islamic history.

Sayyidah al-Farīʿah ﷺ was a Companion of the Prophet ﷺ and the sister of Abū Saʿīd al-Khudrī ﷺ, who was a distinguished Companion of the Prophet ﷺ and renowned for his extensive narration of Hadiths. Abū Saʿīd al-Khudrī ﷺ was not only an extremely knowledgeable man and an authority in Hadith (over a thousand hadiths were narrated by him), but he was also a strong warrior and general for the Muslim army. He was also a political leader, as he had been appointed as the ruler of a province. He held the esteemed position of being a scholar at the Grand Mosque in Medina and his profound knowledge of Hadiths and other domains was widely recognised.

Sayyidah al-Farīʿah had another brother, Qatādah ibn Nuʿmān al-Anṣārī, a strong soldier and warrior who actively participated in the battles of Badr and Uḥud. He is famously remembered for a remarkable incident where, during a conflict, an enemy's strike dislodged his eye. When the Prophet ﷺ saw this, he thrust it back with his hand. Miraculously, after this, Qatādah's vision improved beyond its original state, defying all expectations. This extraordinary occurrence transpired during a battle expedition, demonstrating Qatādah's unwavering commitment and valour.

The father of Sayyidah al-Farīʿah was one of the greatest and foremost Companions of the Prophet ﷺ. The Prophet ﷺ declared that he is one of the people of Paradise. Even though he could not take part in the Battle of Badr, he attained martyrdom by defending the life of the Prophet Muhammad ﷺ in another crucial battle of Muslim history, namely the battle of Uḥud. Her brother, Abū Saʿīd al-Khudrī, was a young child at the time and also wanted to join this battle but the Prophet ﷺ did not allow him to do so because of his young age. Not being able to join the Muslim army made him extremely sad, so when he started weeping, Sayyidah al-Farīʿah embraced him affectionately, wiped his tears, and asked him to patiently wait for the right time. It was at this time that she assumed the role of a motherly figure to her two younger brothers.

After receiving the sad news of their father's death at the Battle of Uḥud, this honourable family stood strong and firm, enduring hardships with patience and bravery. When Sayyidah al-Farīʿah ﷺ heard about her father's martyrdom, she accepted it with equanimity, courage, and patience as advised by the Prophet ﷺ, and also expressed happiness that the Prophet ﷺ returned from the battle safe and sound.

Their father's death left them with no stable source of income. However, they exhibited exemplary patience and avoided seeking any monetary aid. Their strong belief in the advice of the Prophet ﷺ and faith in Allah's help eventually paid off and this family became wealthy and prosperous.

A Source and Authority for the Fiqh of ʿIddah

Sayyidah al-Farīʿah bint Mālik ﷺ was married to Sahl ibn Rāfiʿ ibn Bashīr al-Khazrajī ﷺ, a fellow Anṣārī. However, she experienced the heart-wrenching loss of becoming a young widow when her husband was killed by some of his slaves near Medina. With the grief of losing her husband at such a young age, she decided to return to the house of her parents. However, she first wanted to consult the Prophet ﷺ regarding the permissibility of this course of action. He told her that she should continue to stay in her house until she completed the prescribed waiting period called the ʿiddah (4 months and 10 days), which is required by the Shariah. This directive is explicitly outlined in Sūrah al-Baqarah:

وَالَّذِينَ يُتَوَفَّوْنَ مِنكُمْ وَيَذَرُونَ أَزْوَاجًا يَتَرَبَّصْنَ بِأَنفُسِهِنَّ أَرْبَعَةَ أَشْهُرٍ وَعَشْرًا

'As for those of you who die and leave widows behind, let them observe a waiting period of four months and ten days.'

(al-Baqarah, 2:234)

She followed the Prophet's guidelines and stayed in her house for the prescribed period, after which she devoted her whole life to the service of Islam. Her obedience to the Prophet's counsel exemplifies her unwavering commitment to Islamic teachings and demonstrates her dedication to following the guidance laid out in the Qur'an.

The conditions of al-Farīʿah's ʿiddah later became a precedent for the rules on the ʿiddah for all widowed women, with those studying fiqh in Medina, Syria, Iraq, and Egypt deriving their rulings on the ʿiddah based on her narrations. Muhammad ibn Sīrīn, a prominent scholar known for his narration of dreams, attested to al-Farīʿah's exceptional knowledge and memory, particularly regarding ʿiddah regulations.

He recorded an incident wherein a woman who fell sick after her husband's death was moved to her parents' house so that they could take care of her. When the scholars of the community learnt about this case, they suggested that she should be moved back to her husband's house, as she would need to stay there until the end of her ʿiddah days. She was returned to her husband's home following the directive rooted in the life experiences of Sayyidah al-Farīʿah bint Mālik ﷺ.

Al-Farīʿah bint Mālik's legacy transcended generations, influencing even the great scholars of Islamic jurisprudence, such as Imam Aḥmad ibn Ḥanbal, Imam Abū Ḥanīfah, Imam Mālik, and Imam al-Shāfiʿī. Their adherence to the principles she practiced and taught solidified her impact on Islamic jurisprudence.

The culmination of her influence occurred during the caliphate of Sayyidunā ʿUthmān ibn ʿAffān ﵁, when her expertise was sought in a court case pertaining to a widow during her ʿiddah period. A lady's husband had died, and the matter of her place of residence during the period of her ʿiddah came under consideration. Al-Farīʿah bint Mālik ﵂ was summoned to the court of the Caliph ʿUthmān ibn ʿAffān ﵁. She was asked what the Prophet ﷺ had told her when she was in a similar situation regarding the place where she should pass the ʿiddah period. Her testimony was accepted in the court and applied to the lady.

Remarkable Attributes and Devotion to Islam

Al-Farīʿah bint Mālik was among the select Companions who participated in the Pledge of Riḍwān, the solemn pledge given to the Prophet ﷺ before the Conquest of Mecca, which affirmed her unwavering commitment to obeying the Prophet ﷺ and upholding the cause of Islam.

She was known for her noteworthy attributes and was described as a woman of remarkable diligence, honesty, devotion, intelligence, and memory. These qualities reflect traits that we should all aspire to embody in our lives. Diligence ensures accuracy and precision in our actions, while honesty and devotion are the cornerstones of a righteous character. Her unique strength lay in her ability to internalise the Prophet's teachings swiftly. When she heard a command from the Prophet ﷺ, she promptly absorbed and retained it in her memory. This profound memory served as a valuable resource for scholars who approached her for authentication and reference in the study of traditions and Hadiths. She was particularly distinguished as an authority in matters related to the observance of the ʿiddah. Although she did not directly narrate these teachings, her memory became a reliable guide for scholars seeking to ascertain the authenticity of certain practices.

One such teaching pertains to a Hadith related by Jābir ibn ʿAbdullāh ﷺ, where he asked the Prophet ﷺ about his maternal aunt. He mentioned that his aunt was divorced and wished to prune fruits from her palm trees. A man forbade her to go out, so she went to the Prophet ﷺ seeking his opinion. Al-Farīʿah bint Mālik's account showcases that the Prophet ﷺ granted permission for this action, counteracting the objection of the man who opposed it.

This episode highlights the role of women like al-Farīʿah bint Mālik ﷺ as repositories of knowledge, even in matters as intricate as the ʿiddah. Her own life experiences played a pivotal role in the formation of a significant Islamic ruling, and her actions were instrumental in shaping the course of ʿiddah regulations, which became adopted and endorsed by all four major Islamic schools of thought.

Al-Farīʿah bint Mālik's life story resonates as a testament to the profound impact that a single individual, particularly a woman, can have on the development and preservation of Islamic teachings. Her memory, dedication, and obedience to the Prophet's guidance solidify her as a key figure in Islamic history.

NUSAYBAH BINT KA'B ﵄

The Prophet ﷺ admired her courage and said, 'I did not turn right or left in the battle except that I saw her fighting for me.'

CHAPTER FOUR

Nusaybah bint Kaʿb ﵂

Among the early Muslims were those who pledged allegiance to the Prophet ﷺ after knowing him for only a short while and who vowed to protect him and his fellow migrants at all costs. These people believed in Islam and trusted the integrity of the Prophet ﷺ and welcomed the Meccan Muslims into their community as family, despite hardly knowing them. These people were known as the Anṣār (lit. the Supporters), the people of the blessed land of Medina, and from them hails a great female warrior by the name of Nusaybah bint Kaʿb ﵂.

A Pivotal Role in History

Nusaybah bint Kaʿb ﵂ was an incredible woman whose story is one of courage and strength. She was also known as Umm ʿAmmārah, and was born and raised in Medina amongst the Banu Māzin – a clan from the Khazraj tribe. Sayyidah Nusaybah ﵂ was one of the most prominent female figures in the history of Islam and played a major role in many events.

She was an extraordinary woman with remarkable character traits, such as patience, courage, sincerity, and dedication to faith, with every one of these virtues setting her apart from her peers. She became a Muslim before the Prophet ﷺ migrated to Medina and was one of the two women who travelled with the Companions to meet the Prophet ﷺ in al-ʿAqabah and pledge allegiance to him. It was a memorable event and is remembered as one of the defining moments in the history of Islam. A delegation from Medina went to meet the Prophet ﷺ on the outskirts of Mecca and pledge allegiance to him. The pledge showed the willingness of the people of Medina, namely the Anṣār, to accept the Prophet ﷺ and give him protection and security. They invited him to Medina with honour and respect and looked forward to the blessings this would bring to their people. The Prophet ﷺ believed in them, trusted them, and accepted their invitation. He told them that for the sanctuary they offer and the responsibility they are about to shoulder, Allah ﷻ will grant them nothing less than Paradise. This event changed the course of history and raised Sayyidah Nusaybah and the Anṣār amongst those people beloved to the Prophet ﷺ.

A Brave Warrior

Sayyidah Nusaybah was known for her courage, which she displayed at the time of the Battle of Uḥud. The Muslims had already won the battle, but the disbelievers found a weak spot and attacked again, leading to the defeat of the Muslim army. Sayyidah Nusaybah was on the battlefield at the time, taking care of the wounded, but when she saw that the Prophet ﷺ had been left undefended, she immediately jumped to protect him and bravely started fighting. It is reported that she received 12 wounds that day as she fought to protect the Messenger of Allah ﷺ. Her son, ʿAbdullāh ؓ, was fighting with her when he was struck by a sword. She came to him, wrapped his wound, and told him, 'Go back and continue fighting.' When the Prophet ﷺ saw her encouraging her son to continue fighting despite being severely wounded, he looked at her and said, 'Who can do what you did, O Umm ʿAmmārah!' thereby praising her spirit of sacrifice for Islam.

The Prophet ﷺ saw that the man who had struck her son had come back to the battle and informed her about it. Sayyidah Nusaybah ؓ confronted the fighter, knocked him off his horse, and then killed the man with the help of her other son, Ḥabīb ؓ. The Prophet ﷺ admired her courage and said, 'I did not turn right or left in the battle except that I saw her fighting for me.' Sayyidah Nusaybah ؓ stood strong in the Prophet's defence, obtaining severe wounds in the process. Her courage and bravery are admirable, and with her tireless service earned her a beautiful gift from the Prophet ﷺ, who prayed abundantly for her and her family in the battle. Addressing her son, ʿAbdullāh, the Prophet ﷺ said, 'May Allah ﷻ bless you, O people of this home. Your mother's place is greater than the place of so and so (and he mentioned a Companion).' He then said, 'May Allah ﷻ have mercy on you, O people of this home, and your father's place is greater than the place of so and so.'

Companionship of the Prophet ﷺ

Sayyidah Nusaybah ؓ had a wish, and she asked the Prophet ﷺ to supplicate for her to be his companion in Paradise. Out of all the things in this world that she could ask for him to pray for, she only wanted his companionship – a sign of her integrity and purity. The Prophet ﷺ thus supplicated for her family to be his companions in Paradise.

Sayyidah Nusaybah ﵂ was also one of the women who became a reason for the revelation of a verse of the Qur'an. She came to the Prophet ﷺ one day and asked him, 'The men are taking away all the rewards, and most of the rewards that are mentioned in the Qur'an are about men. What about us women?' The same question was also a concern for Sayyidah Umm Salamah ﵂. The following verse in Sūrah al-Aḥzāb was revealed as an answer to their query:

إِنَّ الْمُسْلِمِينَ وَالْمُسْلِمَاتِ وَالْمُؤْمِنِينَ وَالْمُؤْمِنَاتِ وَالْقَانِتِينَ وَالْقَانِتَاتِ وَالصَّادِقِينَ
وَالصَّادِقَاتِ وَالصَّابِرِينَ وَالصَّابِرَاتِ وَالْخَاشِعِينَ وَالْخَاشِعَاتِ وَالْمُتَصَدِّقِينَ وَالْمُتَصَدِّقَاتِ
وَالصَّائِمِينَ وَالصَّائِمَاتِ وَالْحَافِظِينَ فُرُوجَهُمْ وَالْحَافِظَاتِ وَالذَّاكِرِينَ اللَّهَ كَثِيرًا وَالذَّاكِرَاتِ
أَعَدَّ اللَّهُ لَهُم مَّغْفِرَةً وَأَجْرًا عَظِيمًا

'Surely Muslim men and women, believing men and women, devout men and women, truthful men and women, patient men and women, humble men and women, charitable men and women, fasting men and women, men and women who guard their chastity, and men and women who remember Allah often – for them Allah has prepared forgiveness and a great reward.'

(al-Aḥzāb, 33:35)

A Life of Sacrifice and Bravery

Sayyidah Nusaybah ﵂ also participated in the Conquest of Mecca and the Battle of Yamāmah after the Prophet ﷺ passed away. She was a warrior and an inspiration. Her numerous sacrifices cannot be limited to just one event but spanned over her lifetime, showing how integral women were to the foundation of Islam. She fought for the truth, becoming a shield for the Prophet ﷺ, and left a legacy of courage and selflessness for us all.

CHAPTER FIVE

Umm Sharīk رَضِيَ ٱللَّهُ عَنْهَا

Some of the prominent women who were blessed with the presence of the Prophet ﷺ lived lives that are largely unknown to us. However, the little that we do know stand as powerful examples of faith, determination, and active dedication to Islam. One such woman was Umm Sharīk, or Ghuzayyah bint Jābir ibn Ḥakīm رَضِيَ ٱللَّهُ عَنْهَا – a Companion of the Prophet ﷺ whose story underscores the notion that external factors like name, lineage, and background are inconsequential in the sight of Allah ﷻ.

A Brave Decision

Sayyidah Umm Sharīk's origin and tribe is disputed, but the most common opinion is that she was from the tribe of Daws. Ibn ʿAbbās narrated that Sayyidah Umm Sharīk رَضِيَ ٱللَّهُ عَنْهَا converted to Islam during the early days of Mecca while she was still married to Abū al-ʿAskar al-Dawsī, who was not a Muslim. This brave decision to accept Islam despite her husband's opposition highlights her courage, critical thinking, and ability to challenge the notion of inherited tradition. She did not passively accept the religion of her ancestors, but instead chose the truth with careful analysis, emphasising the great importance of seeking knowledge and developing insight in matters of faith.

Dedicated to Spreading the Message of Islam

After her conversion to Islam, Sayyidah Umm Sharīk ﷺ dedicated herself to calling people to Islam. She would visit the women of Quraysh and invite them to Islam, but when the people of Mecca found out about her mission, they abducted her, threatened her, and forcefully returned her to her tribe. She narrated the events of this journey and said, 'They carried me on a camel without a saddle and left me for three days without water or food. Whenever they stopped somewhere to rest, they would sit under the shade and leave me in the Sun. That was the case until I felt something cold on my chest, so I reached for it and found out that it was a vessel of water. I drank a little bit from it, but it was taken from me and lifted. Then it came back, and I drank from it, but then it was lifted. Then it came back, and I drank from it, but then it was lifted several times. Then it came back, and I drank from it until I was quenched. Then I poured the rest of it on my body and clothes. When they woke up, they saw traces of the water and saw that I looked better. Consequently, they said to me, "You were unchained, so did you take our water and drink from it?" I said, "No, by Allah! What happened was this-and-this." They said, "Indeed, if you are truthful then your religion is better than our religion!" So, they looked for their water and found it just as they had left it. They embraced Islam there and then.' The water was a form of divine provision sent from Allah ﷻ and serves as a reminder that Allah's help is always present for those who strive for His sake.

A Significant Narrator

Sayyidah Umm Sharīk ؓ was also a muḥaddithah, that is, a narrator that reported Hadiths directly from the Prophet ﷺ. Her narration of Hadiths, especially concerning the signs of the Day of Judgment and the appearance of the Dajjāl, illustrates her role as a transmitter of knowledge and her direct connection to the teachings of the Prophet ﷺ. In one narration, she said that the Prophet ﷺ ordered her to kill a chameleon, a kind of lizard that was called al-wazagh. He said that it blew on the fire that was ignited for Prophet Ibrāhīm ؑ, and because of its harmful nature, it is one of the animals that is allowed to be killed.

In another narration, Sayyidunā Jābir ibn 'Abdullāh ؓ, who was one of the major Companions of the Prophet ﷺ, said that Umm Sharīk ؓ told him that she heard the Prophet ﷺ say that people will run away from the Dajjāl, seeking shelter in the mountains. When she asked him if there will be Arabs at that time or if people would defend themselves, he replied that they will be very small in number.

Sayyidah Umm Sharīk's legacy, characterised by her commitment to spreading Islam and enduring trials, offers numerous lessons for Muslims today. Her sacrifices and honourable actions inspire us to live with integrity.

CHAPTER SIX

Al-Rubayyiʿ bint Muʿawwidh ﵂

Out of the many stories from our glorious Islamic history that deserve to be told, some have a special place due to their impact. These are the stories of women who persevered in the face of adversities, found strength in their faith, and turned their lives into an example of courage and resilience. One such woman with exemplary character was al-Rubayyiʿ bint Muʿawwidh ﵂, a Companion of the Prophet ﷺ, muḥaddithah, and a role model to women of all generations.

A Noble Status

Sayyidah al-Rubayyiʿ bint Muʿawwidh ﵂ came from a well-known family of Companions. She was an Anṣārī woman born in Medina and belonged to the Khazraj tribe. She was the daughter of a noble Companion, Sayyidunā Muʿawwidh ibn al-Ḥārith ﵁, who was killed in the Battle of Badr. Her two paternal uncles, Sayyidunā Muʿādh ibn ʿAfrāʾ and Sayyidunā ʿAwf ibn ʿAfrāʾ ﵄, were also actively involved in the Battle of Badr. The Prophet ﷺ prayed for them, and they were included in the second pledge of al-ʿAqabah. Her sister, Sayyidah ʿUmayrah bint Muʿawwidh ﵂, was also a Muslim.

Sayyidah al-Rubayyi' bint Mu'awwidh 🌸 was married to a prominent businessman, Ayās ibn Bakīr and had only one son, Muhammad ibn Ayās. She was also a muḥaddithah and narrated a total of twenty important Hadiths directly from the Prophet 🌸. Some of the most famous scholars of Islam narrated Hadiths that she transmitted, including 'Āʾishah bint Anas ibn Mālik, Sulaymān ibn Yasār, Khālid ibn Dhakwān, 'Abdullāh ibn Muhammad ibn 'Aqīl, and Abū 'Ubaydah Muhammad ibn 'Ammār ibn Yāsir.

Marriage

A profound Hadith narrated by Sayyidah al-Rubayyiʿ bint Muʿawwidh 🌸 gives us an insight into how marriages were celebrated at the time of the Prophet 🌸 and the permissible actions on this occasion. Sayyidah al-Rubayyiʿ narrated the following:

'After the consummation of my marriage, the Prophet 🌸 came and sat on my bed as far from me as you are sitting now, and our little girls started beating the tambourines and reciting elegiac verses mourning my father who had been killed in the battle of Badr. One of them said, "Among us is a Prophet who knows what will happen tomorrow." On that, the Prophet 🌸 said, "Leave this (saying) and keep on saying the verses which you had been saying before."'

(al-Bukhārī)

The Hadith mentions that when the Prophet 🌸 visited her on the night of her marriage, some girls were singing while playing on the daff (instrument). The Prophet 🌸 was enjoying their singing, until they mentioned in their song that the Prophet 🌸 knows the unseen (ghayb). He stopped them and said that he does not know the unknown and that only Allah 🕮 knows the ghayb, so they continued with their singing while excluding that line.

Khul

Another vital Hadith that was transmitted to us through Sayyidah al-Rubayyiʿ was about the waiting period for khulʿ – the type of divorce which is requested by the wife. It is reported that after the death of the Prophet 🕮 and during the caliphate of ʿUthmān ibn ʿAffān 🕮, Sayyidah al-Rubayyiʿ 🕮 developed some differences with her husband, so she sought a khulʿ as she did not want to be his wife anymore; in return, she would give him everything she had. Her husband agreed and took everything with him. She went to Sayyidunā ʿUthmān ibn ʿAffān 🕮 and asked about the waiting period she needed to observe, and he informed her that she did not have to observe any waiting period unless she had intercourse with him recently. In that case, she would have to stay with him until her next menstruation.

ʿUthmān ibn ʿAffān 🕮 followed the ruling that the Prophet 🕮 gave during his lifetime to a female Companion who faced a situation of domestic abuse at the hands of her husband. Jamīlah bint ʿAbdullāh ibn Ubayy 🕮 was hit by her husband, Thābit ibn Qays ibn Shammās, and as a result, her arm was broken. She came to the Prophet 🕮, and he gave her the ruling for khulʿ.

Ibn ʿAbbās narrated in this regard:

The wife of Thābit ibn Qays came to the Prophet 🕮 and said, "O Allah's Messenger! I do not blame Thābit for defects in his character or his religion, but I, being a Muslim, dislike to behave in an un-Islamic manner (if I remain with him)." On that, Allah's Messenger 🕮 said (to her), "Will you give back the garden which your husband has given you (as mahr)?" She said, "Yes." Then the Prophet ﷺ said to Thābit, "O Thābit! Accept your garden, and divorce her once."'

(al-Bukhārī)

In cases where the husband divorces his wife, the waiting period for her is three menstrual cycles, after which she can accept a proposal and get married again. However, if a wife seeks a khulʿ in return for her dowry, she does not have to wait before getting married again unless she had intercourse with her husband recently. In the latter case, she should wait until after her menstrual cycle in order to confirm that she is not pregnant. This insight into Islamic jurisprudence sheds light on a vital aspect of divorce proceedings, especially for women.

Narrating the Ablution of the Prophet ﷺ

Al-Rubayyiʿ bint Muʿawwidh ﵂ was also honoured to learn the Sunnah of the Prophet ﷺ whenever he would visit her. One of the most important Hadiths that she narrated was regarding the Prophet's method of making wuḍū'. Al-Rubayyiʿ bint Muʿawwidh ﵂ would provide water to the Prophet ﷺ herself and watch him make ablution. She would pour water for him, and he would offer prayers, have a meal, and then rest for a while. Many Companions asked her to relate to them the Hadiths of the Prophet ﷺ on the basis of the knowledge she gained directly from him. The command for making wuḍū' came to us through the Qur'an, but it was through her narration of the Prophet's action that we received the exact manner of doing so. She took the opportunity to memorise it and share it with the Companions so that it would benefit Muslims forever.

Al-Rubayyiʿ bint Muʿawwidh 🌸 narrated the way that the Prophet 🌸 made wuḍūʾ and said, 'He would wash his hands three times, then wash his face three times. He would rinse his mouth once and clean his nose by drawing in water. Next, he washed his arms up to the elbows three times. Then he would wipe his head by drawing his palms over from the front of his forehead to the back of the nape of his neck, then back to the forehead. Then he would insert his fingers into the outer and inner parts of his ears. Then he washed each foot three times.'

We also know and appreciate the Prophet's appearance today thanks to her descriptions of his blessed face. For example, Abū ʿUbaydah ibn Muhammad ibn ʿAmmār ibn Yāsir once asked al-Rubayyiʿ bint Muʿawwidh 🌸 to describe how the Prophet 🌸 looked, and she answered that he looked as bright as the Sun.

The Fast of ʿĀshūrāʾ and the Pledge of al-Riḍwān

Sayyidah al-Rubayyiʿ 🌸 was also the source of another crucial Hadith that pertains to our worship: fasting on the Day of ʿĀshūrāʾ. Al-Rubayyiʿ bint Muʿawwidh 🌸 narrated:

'The Prophet 🌸 sent a messenger to the village of the Anṣār in the morning of the day of ʿĀshūrāʾ (10th of Muḥarram) to announce: "Whoever has eaten something should not eat but complete the fast, and whoever is observing the fast should complete it."' She further said, 'Since then, we used to fast on that day regularly and also make our boys fast. We used to make toys of wool for the boys and if anyone of them cried for food, he was given those toys till it was the time of the breaking of the fast.'

(al-Bukhārī)

Serving the Prophet ﷺ and the Community

Al-Rubayyiʿ bint Muʿawwidh ﷺ had the honour of exchanging gifts with the Prophet ﷺ. She was much respected by him ﷺ, and he would happily accept the gifts she gave to him. She would serve him his favourite dishes whenever he would visit her, and he also gifted her with some gold and silver ornaments he received from Bahrain, asking her to wear them. She says in a narration, 'I brought the Prophet ﷺ a tray of ripe dates and fluffy cucumber, so he gave me a handful of ornaments', or she said, 'of gold'. This Hadith shows the munificence of the Messenger of Allah ﷺ and teaches us that we should acknowledge people for their hospitality.

She was a woman of courage and foresight and strived constantly for the cause of Allah ﷻ. She was an active member of Medinan society, providing relief to the soldiers during wars and bandaging and nursing the wounded. Al-Bukhārī mentions a narration by her in which she says, 'We used to go for military expeditions along with Allah's Messenger ﷺ and provided the people with water, served them, and brought the dead and the wounded back to Medina.' This Hadith illustrates that a woman can tend to a wounded man and vice versa in times of necessity.

Another remarkable thing about this wonderful woman is that she was a part of the congregation that took the oath of allegiance in the 6th year of the Hijrah, which became celebrated in Islamic history as the Pledge of al-Riḍwān. Moreover, she heard about her entrance to Paradise in the Hereafter from the lips of the Prophet ﷺ himself, who said, 'Whosoever participated in the Pledge of al-Riḍwān are the holders of Paradise.'

Sayyidah al-Rubayyiʿ ﷺ passed away in the 45th year of the Hijrah during the caliphate of Muʿāwiyah ibn Abī Sufyān ﷺ, leaving behind a legacy of servitude and dedication to Islam. She left a mark on those who knew her and learned from her, living a life of faith and patience. Her modest number of narrated Hadiths were of insurmountable value and serve as a profound reminder of the invaluable contributions that women made to the early Islamic community, demonstrating that the impact of one's contributions transcend quantity.

SUMAYYAH BINT KHAYYĀṬ ﵂

Her sacrifice and strength in the face of persecution is one of the most memorable chapters in the history of Islam.

CHAPTER SEVEN

Sumayyah bint Khayyāṭ رضي الله عنها

Those who accepted Islam in its early days were some of the most tested and resilient Muslims. Their actions and sacrifices inspired many others who followed their example and found the strength to stand firm against falsehood. One of the most profound of such people was Sayyidah Sumayyah bint Khayyāṭ رضي الله عنها, the first female martyr of Islam.

Defined by her Qualities

Sumayyah bint Khayyāṭ رضي الله عنها was an Abyssinian slave woman with exceptional manners and admirable qualities. She lived in Mecca at the time of the Prophet ﷺ and was an extremely intelligent woman who was known for making sensible decisions in every situation. She had the wisdom to choose the right words and actions at the right time, demonstrated patience when needed, and showed remarkable courage in the face of adversity. It was these qualities and the way she carried herself respectably that made people respect her notwithstanding her social status as a slave. This serves as a reminder to us that our true identity is not determined solely by external factors or what others say about us but by our character, actions, and the values we hold dear.

Sayyidah Sumayyah bint Khayyāṭ رضي الله عنها was a slave to Abū

Ḥudhayfah and married Sayyidunā Yāsir ibn ʿĀmir رضي الله عنه, who was his servant. They lived in the same house, and after their marriage, Abū Ḥudhayfah decided to free them both and let them go. However, they chose to remain within the household and continue working to please Allah ﷻ.

Their marriage was a happy one, and Sayyidah Sumayyah رضي الله عنها soon gave birth to a son, whom they named ʿAmmār ibn Yāsir رضي الله عنه. Abū Ḥudhayfah insisted on freeing them from bondage, and even after they became free, he maintained good relations with them, helping them financially whenever they needed. They had two more sons after this, named ʿAbdullāh and Ḥarth. Tragically, Ḥarth met an untimely death before the dawn of Islam, and it was soon after that this small happy family entered a period of unending trials.

Illuminated by the Light of Islam

Sayyidunā ʿAmmār ibn Yāsir رضي الله عنه was the first in their family to accept Islam, and his mother followed him in this noble act. Sayyidah Sumayyah رضي الله عنها was one of the first seven people to accept the message of Islam. In her wisdom and at 60 years old, her age did not stop her from recognising the truth and accepting it. Her husband also became a Muslim shortly after, and the family would go to the Prophet ﷺ together to learn from him, concealing their faith from the non-believers.

The light of Islam began flourishing in their home, with Sayyidah Sumayyah رضي الله عنها holding the reigns of the family and shaping their character according to the Prophet's teachings. These were the early days of Islam, when there were very few Muslims in Mecca, and those who did become Muslim concealed it in public. Abū Ḥudhayfah, who was once a benevolent master to them, turned to cruelty and torture. He was a leader of one of the tribes in Mecca, and began tormenting the family by beating and imprisoning them. However, they stood firm against this inhumane treatment and did not give in to the disbelievers.

Standing Firm Against Torture

Sayyidah Sumayyah and her family were tortured in unimaginable ways by Abū Ḥudhayfah and Abū Jahl, who was also a leader of one of the tribes in Mecca. Abū Jahl was a tyrant and one of the most severe enemies of Islam, who took it upon himself to make this family suffer. He took them to the desert, tied their hands and feet to wooden poles, and tortured them in the blazing Sun. He then left them in the desert of Mecca without any provision. Coerced into denouncing their faith under merciless conditions, Sayyidah Sumayyah and her family remained steadfast and patient.

This torment occurred during the advent of Islam, when the Prophet ﷺ and the Companions did not have the resources or strength to protect the early Muslims from the powerful leaders of Mecca. Most of those who had accepted Islam kept it hidden out of fear of persecution. The Prophet ﷺ was also in a weak position at the time, and when he would pass by them, he would weep and say words of encouragement to them. His famous words, 'Be patient, O family of Yāsir, your destination is Jannah', remain etched in history. This statement by the Messenger of Allah ﷺ was a glad tiding for the blessed family as they staunchly rejected the attempts of the disbelievers to make them give up their faith.

The First Female Martyr

In an act of unimaginable cruelty, Abū Jahl eventually took a spear and stabbed Sayyidah Sumayyah ﵂, causing her to die instantly and become the first female martyr of Islam. Sayyidah Sumayyah ﵂ was not a woman of great knowledge. She had not memorised the entire Qur'an or learned the different spheres of Islamic law, but her sacrifice and strength in the face of persecution is one of the most memorable chapters in the history of Islam. Abū Jahl wanted to make an example out of Sayyidah Sumayyah ﵂ and put fear in the hearts of the believers. Instead, it made their hearts stronger and filled them with the strength of unshakable faith. Her death and sacrifices were not in vain, as the whole of Mecca now saw the power of the truth.

Sayyidah Sumayyah's biggest strength was her conviction and belief in Allah ﷻ. She was a woman of action and practised what she learned. Her focus was on the Hereafter and the pleasure of Allah ﷻ, and she was willing to sacrifice her life in this world for the eternal life of Paradise. There is not much more that is known about her, but what little we know is enough to put her among the top few female Companions who became an example of resilience and strength.

Sayyidah Sumayyah's legacy became an emblem of strength, courage, and the unyielding power of faith in action. She is a role model for Muslim women who find themselves tested in faith and life and has transcended the bounds of her time and place, becoming an everlasting source of inspiration for generations to come.

CHAPTER EIGHT

Rufaydah al-Aslamiyyah ﵂

At the time of the Prophet ﷺ, there was a woman who pioneered medical care for her community and brought medical relief to the battlefield – a contribution so significant to the well-being of the Muslim community that she will be forever remembered as a pioneer of Islamic health care. Rufaydah al-Aslamiyyah ﵂ was a Companion of the Prophet ﷺ, the first Muslim nurse, and social activist. Her story is one of service to others.

Early Exposure to Medicine

Rufaydah al-Aslamiyyah ﵂ was one of the first people in Medina to accept Islam, and she participated actively in welcoming the Prophet ﷺ to Medina when he migrated from Mecca. Sayyidah Rufaydah ﵂ was born in 620 CE and belonged to the Banū Aslam tribe. Her father, Saʿd al-Aslamī, was a surgeon and physician, and as she grew up watching him and learning from him, he became her biggest mentor and teacher. She gained her early exposure to medical science through him, and with dedication and commitment, became a highly skilled medic.

The books of Muslims and non-Muslims alike describe her simply – yet profoundly – as an expert healer. She became a well-known physician of her time, and her expertise, coupled with a stellar character, blessed her treatment with a healing power that was unique. She used her knowledge to be of service to her community, and her passion for bringing relief to people became especially useful during the times of combat.

A Medic on the Battlefield

Sayyidah Rufaydah رضي الله عنها provided relief to the soldiers of prominent battles, including Badr, Uḥud, and Khandaq. In an effort to take care of the soldiers in these battles, she took permission from the Prophet ﷺ along with some volunteers to set up medical camps on the battlefield, an act that was greatly appreciated and honoured by the Prophet ﷺ. After the Battle of Badr, she established what can be regarded as an early military hospital in the Prophet's mosque, keeping it equipped with beds, bandages, and medicine. During the Battle of Uḥud, the number of wounded increased greatly, so she decided to establish a field hospital with a system of movable tents to be as close to the injured as possible and give them the proper treatment they needed. As her tent became full of patients, she invited other women to help her run the hospital. It is narrated that Sayyidah Umm Sulaym, Sayyidah Ā'ishah bint Abī Bakr, and Sayyidah Umm Salīṭ al-Anṣāriyyah رضي الله عنهن helped her in the process of healing the wounded during the Battle of Uḥud.

Sayyidah Rufaydah رضي الله عنها was known for her tent, which did not just serve as a hospital but became a shelter from the heat and wind of the harsh desert. She was a charismatic and capable leader who pioneered a holistic system of medical care for her Muslim community, and her incredible focus on hygiene is remembered as one of the most exceptional aspects of her medical expertise and insight. The Prophet 🌼 trusted the nursing abilities of Sayyidah Rufaydah 🌼 and relied on her for the treatment of his beloved Companions. This is evident from his order for Sayyidunā Saʿd ibn Muʿādh 🌼 at the time of the Battle of Khandaq. Sayyidunā Saʿd ibn Muʿādh 🌼 was heavily wounded in this battle, so the Prophet 🌼 immediately ordered for him to be carried to Rufaydah's tent, who was operating a diligent medical care unit throughout the battle. When the battle ended, the tribe of Banū Qurayẓah surrendered on the condition that Sayyidunā Saʿd ibn Muʿādh 🌼 would determine their fate and not the Prophet 🌼. Since he was still heavily injured and could not walk, he was carried from Rufaydah's tent under her supervision, and after administering his ruling on Banū Qurayẓah, was returned to the tent.

A Mentor for Young Women

It is recorded that Sayyidah Rufaydah 🌼 successfully ran the first-ever documented mobile care unit that was able to meet the medical needs of the community, setting up an example of determination, hard work, and willingness to be of service. She was not only passionate about nursing but also about teaching other women to treat the injured and sick. She also shared her knowledge with women who were willing to nurse; since she would give treatment to her patients, she would have volunteers watch and learn from her. Her vision was to equip more women with the skills needed to continue the noble work of providing relief and care.

Even after the battles, she continued her healthcare practice by taking care of the general public. To help more people utilise her services, she maintained a small clinic near the Prophet's Mosque, where she would train nurses and treat her patients. Sayyidah Rufaydah ؓ also designed codes of ethics for medical care and nursing and was an advocate for health education, health care, and disease prevention.

Honoured and Rewarded for Her Service

The Prophet ﷺ recognised her contributions and endless service to the community and honoured her for her participation in the battles by gifting her a share of the bounties of war, which was equal to the provisions allotted to the soldiers who fought. It was a well-deserved prize for her undying dedication and courage on the battlefield.

To commemorate her contributions and motivate medical students, the Royal College of Surgeons in Ireland and the University of Bahrain present the coveted and prestigious al-Rufaida al-Aslamiya Prize in Nursing each year. This award, determined by a panel of senior clinical personnel and medical staff members, is given to one student every year who consistently and dedicatedly provides exceptional nursing care to patients.

Rufaydah al-Aslamiyyah ؓ remains a luminary, illuminating the path of selfless service for generations to come. Her legacy inspires us to strive for excellence in whatever we do, no matter how small one's objectives may be. She dedicated her life to the development of nursing and medical health, leaving behind a wealth of knowledge that continues to benefit us today.

PART THREE

Female Pioneers of Islamic History

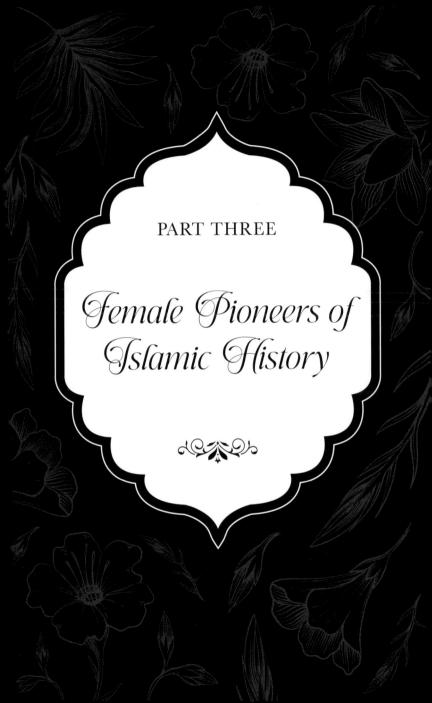

These women all shared a common vision: to make their children a beacon of knowledge and guidance so that they could attain a close status with Allah ﷻ

CHAPTER ONE

Ḥafṣah bint Sīrīn ﷺ

After the death of the Prophet ﷺ, Islam continued to spread to faraway lands and accumulated great scholars and teachers from around the world. Among these scholars were women who transcended the boundaries of social and economic status and left a legacy of remarkable knowledge and wisdom.

A Desire for Knowledge

Ḥafṣah bint Sīrīn was born in Basra, Iraq, in the 30th year of the Hijrah (650 CE). Her captivating story starts with a humble childhood. She belonged to a slave family, with her father being a slave of Sayyidunā Anas ibn Mālik and her mother being a freed slave from Sayyidunā Abū Bakr. Owing to this, she grew up under limited means with many brothers and sisters. The most renowned of them was Muhammad ibn Sīrīn, who was a famous scholar with knowledge of the field of dream interpretation.

Sayyidah Ḥafṣah grew up with an intense desire to learn, and by the age of 12, she had memorised the entire Qur'an. Most remarkably, she also learned the in-depth meanings of the Qur'an, which included knowledge of tafsīr (Quranic interpretation) and qirā'āt (different recitation ſtyles). She gained such command in this field that she became a reliable reference of knowledge for many later scholars. Her brother, Muhammad ibn Sīrīn 🙏, who was a learned scholar himself, would consult her on various issues.

Imam Ibn al-Jawzī 🙏 commented about Sayyidah Ḥafṣah bint Sīrīn in his famous book Ṣifah al-Ṣafwah by ſtating, 'Categorically, I have not seen anyone from the Followers more knowledgeable than Ḥafṣah bint Sīrīn.' He was asked, 'Not even al-Ḥasan al-Baṣrī or her brother Muhammed?' And he said, 'No'.

As a ſtudent of Sayyidunā Anas ibn Mālik 🙏, Sayyidah Ḥafṣah's thirſt for knowledge was relentless. In his famous book al-Muhaddithat, an encyclopaedia about the female scholars of Hadith, Shaykh Akram Nadwi mentions her and acknowledges her vaſt knowledge. He says, 'Although she was a slave, she used all the opportunities that Allah 🙏 gave her to learn, to be knowledgeable and to spread knowledge.'

She narrated many Hadiths, and a prominent one describing how to wash the body of a dead person was narrated solely by her. Her chain of narration was from Umm 'Aṭiyyah 🙏, who was a Companion. She was also a juriſt. Her deep underſtanding of the Qur'an and its interpretations, coupled with her expertise in Hadith and fiqh, positioned her as an authority among scholars and seekers of knowledge.

A Life of Detachment

The book Ṣifah al-Ṣafwah documents Sayyidah Ḥafṣah's extensive acts of worship and devotion. It is described that sometimes she would be engaged in prayer from the time of Ẓuhr until ʿIshā' whereby she would not leave her space of prayer.

She was a well-known ascetic and lived a life of self-discipline with just the minimum, refraining from indulging in the trivialities of the world. The concept of living with detachment from worldly desires and always being prepared for the next life was an integral part of her character. She would evaluate herself constantly and believed that she was not doing enough to please Allah ﷻ. She had a helper in her house, and the helper was once asked, 'How was Ḥafṣah?' She said, 'She was always crying, she was amazing, and she cried a lot in her worship.' Seeing her cry constantly and always evaluating herself, the helper thought that Sayyidah Ḥafṣah must have done something major to make her so remorseful and sad. But the beauty of her thoughts and character was unimaginable, and her reasons for crying were not conceivable by any. When asked for the reason, she replied, 'I live and I know that I am going to die any minute, and I am worried that when I die, I will not be ready to meet my Lord.' What extraordinary faith she had that despite her level of worship and fear of Allah ﷻ, she felt that she was not ready to meet Him.

Remembering the Destroyer of Pleasures

An interesting fact about Sayyidah Ḥafṣah ؓ is that she carried her burial shroud, namely her kafan, with her. When she went for ʿUmrah and Hajj, she used this cloth, and it was always with her wherever she went. It is said that she would even sleep in it in case death came while she was sleeping. Here we can see her cultivating the habit of remembering death and embracing the famous aphorism of our Prophet ﷺ, who said, 'Remember frequently death, the thing that cuts off pleasures' (al-Tirmidhī, 2307).

Sayyidah Ḥafṣah lived a simple life and died in an even simpler way in the year 719 CE. Her sole focus and goal was the Hereafter, and she lived in the world as a wayfarer in a temporary abode. The legacy of Ḥafṣah bint Sīrīn reminds us that those who dedicate their life to seeking knowledge and deepening one's connection with Allah ﷻ are the ones who are ultimately successful. Her story serves as an encouragement for us all, regardless of our circumstances, to strive for excellence in faith and understanding.

CHAPTER TWO

The Mother of Imam al-Bukhārī ﷺ

We often discuss the remarkable achievements of prominent scholars and people of knowledge and the transformations they brought to our ummah, but rarely do we discuss the inspiration behind them. When we carefully explore the history of Islam, we find that many scholars were supported by strong women throughout their lives.

Interestingly, many of the prominent scholars of Islam were raised by single mothers, who nurtured them, disciplined them, and gave them the direction needed to become noble, pious, and character-strong men. These women all shared a common vision: to make their children a beacon of knowledge and guidance so that they could attain a close status with Allah ﷻ. For this vision, they worked tirelessly.

Raising an Icon of Knowledge

Abū ʿAbdullāh Muhammad ibn Ismāʿīl al-Bukhārī ﷺ or more simply Imam al-Bukhārī was a scholar of Hadith. He is most famously known for his canonical Hadith compilation al-Jāmiʿ al-Musnad al-Ṣaḥīḥ, which is colloquially referred to as Ṣaḥīḥ al-Bukhārī. Imam al-Bukhārī's father was also a well-known scholar of Hadith who travelled all over the world to gain knowledge, but he passed away quite young, leaving behind a young son under the sole care of his mother. It is interesting to note that we do not know the name of Imam al-Bukhārī's mother, but what is well-known about her is that she did a huge favour for the Muslim ummah by preparing her son to become one of the most widely recognised scholars of all time.

Imam al-Bukhārī's mother ﷺ had plans for him, and she wanted him to become like his father. However, when Imam al-Bukhārī ﷺ reached the age of 12, Allah ﷻ tested him with a medical condition, and he lost his sight. His mother took him to several physicians and tried many remedies, but nothing worked. From then on, she started spending nights in prayer, making duʿā' with the full conviction that Allah ﷻ would restore his sight. She embraced Allah's words:

وَقَالَ رَبُّكُمُ ادْعُونِي أَسْتَجِبْ لَكُم

'Ask Me, implore to Me, supplicate to Me, and I will respond.'

(Ghāfir, 40:60)

An Answered Prayer

Imam al-Bukhārī's mother ﷺ continued praying, hoping for Allah's help to come soon. She was persistent and determined, and sure enough, Allah ﷻ answered her prayers. She had a dream in which Sayyidunā Ibrāhīm ﷺ came to her and told her that her son will start seeing again. Shortly after, Allah ﷻ restored Imam al-Bukhārī's eyesight as a result of his mother's sincere supplication and trust in His mercy.

During the years of his blindness, Imam al-Bukhārī's mother ﵀ did not let go of her mission to educate her son and teach him about Islam. By the time Imam al-Bukhārī could see again, he had accumulated a lot of knowledge from his mother, who would read him Hadiths of the Prophet ﷺ along with their chains of transmission. Imam al-Bukhārī was so sharp and intelligent that he recorded and memorised a substantial number of these reports. Through hard work and dedication, his mother instilled a deep appreciation for Hadith and Islamic knowledge in her son. As such, every Hadith and piece of information that Imam al-Bukhārī left for us can be accredited to his mother.

When Imam al-Bukhārī ﵀ regained his sight, his mother ﵀ encouraged him to learn even more. While al-Bukhārī was just 18 years old, she took him and his brother on Hajj and left him in Mecca so that he could learn directly from knowledgeable scholars.

A Continuous Charity

The influence of Imam al-Bukhārī's mother ﵀ extends far beyond her son, as he went on to mentor and teach scholars like Imam Muslim and Imam al-Tirmidhī. The story of Imam al-Bukhārī's mother serves as an inspiration for mothers everywhere. Such tremendous sacrifice, determination, and hard work cannot go to waste, and it is the promise of Allah ﷻ that those who walk in His path will find Him running toward them. This mother is a shining example of just that. Her unwavering faith and efforts remind us that the role of a mother goes beyond the immediate care and comfort of her child. It involves cultivating a strong foundation of faith, knowledge, and character that will shape the child's future and allow them to contribute positively to society.

CHAPTER THREE

Fāṭimah bint ʿAbdullāh al-Azdiyyah ﷺ

The Mother of Imam al-Shāfiʿī ﷺ

The collective knowledge of our religion that we are blessed to have access to is not just a result of the work of well-known scholars and teachers, but also the hard work and vision of the people behind them. The biographies of many of these people are relatively obscure, but their actions have left such a mark on history that their legacy will always be present. One such figure is Fāṭimah bint ʿAbdullāh al-Azdiyyah ﷺ, the mother of the prominent scholar Imam al-Shāfiʿī ﷺ, who laid the groundwork for all his achievements and accomplishments.

Dedication and Sacrifice

Imam al-Shāfiʿī ﷺ was one of the foremost scholars of Islam and also the founder of one of the four Sunni schools of thought. He is especially known to have made a significant contribution to the development of a new science known as uṣūl al-fiqh (the roots of jurisprudence). Besides being a great scholar of knowledge, he was also an authority in poetry and lineage.

Imam al-Shāfiʿī grew up as an orphan. His father died soon after his birth, and his mother, Fāṭimah bint ʿAbdullāh al-Azdiyyah, faced many challenges and financial constraints. Instead of remarrying, Fāṭimah decided to devote herself to her young son. Allah had given him a special gift, and seeing the enormous potential and intelligence he possessed, she decided to dedicate her time and effort to facilitating her son's educational journey.

Fāṭimah wanted her son to attain the most authentic knowledge and learn from the best scholars, so the first step on their journey took them from Palestine to Mecca in search of this objective. In these times and given the difficulties of transportation, moving from one place to another was a life-changing decision. It was even more unimaginable for a single mother with a young son. However, Fāṭimah believed wholeheartedly in the cause she had dedicated her life to and took on the challenges that came. She knew that it demanded sacrifice and tolerance and as a result she embarked on the long journey for the sake of Allah.

Overcoming Financial Hardship

Fāṭimah was very poor, and it is reported that she could not afford to send Imam al-Shāfiʿī to school or buy him basic resources. It is narrated that when Imam al-Shāfiʿī once came to her, asking her to buy him some paper so that he could write and record information, she said, 'I do not have it, but let us work on your memory so you can use your memory as paper.'

Fāṭimah's willpower was strong, and she had such high aspirations for her son that nothing could deter her from her goals. She did not allow the lack of resources to limit him and encouraged him to focus on his own faculties. It is reported that Imam al-Shāfiʿī had a photographic memory and was extraordinarily intelligent – talents that were nurtured by the hard work, encouragement, and support of his mother.

Fāṭimah did not have much money, but whatever she had, she used it to help her son learn. One day, Imam al-Shāfiʿī told his mother that the teachers were not taking him seriously because he was not a paying student, and the advice his mother gave him shows her incredible determination. Fāṭimah did not become discouraged nor did she let her son lose confidence. Instead, she gave him sound advice, telling him to display his ability, outperform expectations, and help other students. She advised him that if his dedication was visible, their approach with him would change. With renewed determination and focus, Imam al-Shāfiʿī followed her advice, and it did not take long before they accepted him with a full scholarship.

Imam Ibn Ḥajar describes Fāṭimah as a woman of great worship and devotion who played a central role in Imam al-Shāfiʿī's life. She was the biggest contributor to his achievements, and her great vision shaped his character, making him a person of high integrity and dignity. Her beautiful character was an inspiration for him, allowing him to become the respectable student and teacher he was.

A Woman of Knowledge

Fāṭimah ؓ was also a woman of knowledge herself, and one famous story illustrates just how educated she was. On one occasion, a judge invited Fāṭimah to the court for testimony, along with another woman. When the women were divided in opinion, she was called to the court alone to give her testimony. Upon arriving, she pointed out the error that the judge had made in calling her alone, citing the verse from the Qur'an that mandates the testimony of two women to be considered acceptable. From this, we can derive a key moral lesson: in order to give an educational upbringing to our children, we need to educate ourselves first.

Fāṭimah bint ʿAbdullāh al-Azdiyyah ؓ was a mother who deserves to be remembered among the best of people. She demonstrated that building a nation, namely an ummah, requires not only the efforts of well-known figures but also the dedication of individuals behind the scenes. For the latter are the ones who tirelessly support, nurture, and guide those who go on to shape the future. Hers is a story of sacrifice, the sacrifice of worldly benefit in exchange for a successful investment in the eternal future.

MOTHER OF IMAM AḤMAD ﷺ

Her dedication, sacrifice, and determination to nurture both religious and practical knowledge to her progeny, played a pivotal role in cultivating Imam Aḥmad's exceptional qualities

CHAPTER FOUR

Ṣafiyyah bint Maymūnah bint ʿAbd al-Malik al-Shaybāniyyah رحمها الله

The Mother of Imam Aḥmad ibn Ḥanbal رحمه الله

Another woman who made immense sacrifices and left a mark on the history of Islam was the mother of a great scholar, Imam Aḥmad ibn Ḥanbal رحمه الله – a well-known jurist, narrator of Hadith, Imam, and expert in the Arabic language and the Qur'an. Imam Aḥmad ibn Ḥanbal's teacher, Imam al-Shāfiʿī رحمه الله, said about him, 'When I left Baghdad, I left a man who is a leader in seven disciplines of knowledge.' He was a leader who not only excelled in the Sunnah, Qur'an, and fiqh but also in his good character. He lived a life of asceticism and piety, and behind all these characteristics and achievements was his mother, who guided him and laid the foundation for his love of knowledge.

Laying the Foundation of Piety

Ṣafiyyah bint Maymūnah al-Shaybāniyyah رحمها الله, the mother of Imam Aḥmad ibn Ḥanbal رحمه الله, came from a very good lineage and grew up privileged. Her father was from Banū Shaybān, which went back to Banū ʿĀmir, and her grandfather was a nobleman. She got married when she was young and delivered her son, Aḥmad. Her husband died at a young age, leaving her a widow in her late 20s. Just like the mother of Imam al-Shāfiʿī ﷺ, she refused to remarry and decided to focus on bringing up her son to become a knowledgeable and pious person. As a young widow and single mother, Ṣafiyyah ﷺ faced numerous challenges. But thanks to her dedication, sacrifice, and determination to nurture both religious and practical knowledge to her progeny, she played a pivotal role in cultivating Imam Aḥmad's exceptional qualities.

She began training Aḥmad from childhood, and maintained a disciplined routine to structure his day. He described his day by saying, 'My mother used to wake me up before Fajr. I was about ten years of age and she would warm the water for me before I was up. We would both make wuḍū' and pray until the time of Fajr.' At just ten, she had already established the love of ṣalāh in his heart. After that, she would take him to the mosque to pray Fajr and stay with him. There were usually classes or study circles after Fajr, and she would stay with him until he finished the classes before taking him back home.

Ṣafiyyah's determination to educate her son also extended beyond religious studies. She imparted to him knowledge of language, history, and the characteristics of Arab nobility. She was his first mentor. Imam Aḥmad ﷺ said, 'She was not just my mother, for she was also my teacher. She taught me language and the Qur'an. She taught me history and she taught me all that I needed to know about Arab nobility. But, above that, and this is because we did not have the means to live comfortably, she taught me how to be patient and live with very little.'

A New Chapter

Since giving birth, Ṣafiyyah's entire life had revolved around her son. She was a widow living under difficult circumstances who had invested her time and effort into her son's education and had a clear vision for him. Thus, when Imam Aḥmad رحمه الله completed his studies in Baghdad, it was with a heavy heart that she knew the next chapter of his life must begin. In search of wider knowledge and experience, Ṣafiyyah sent her son to Mecca, Medina, and Yemen. As parting words, she said to her son, 'O son, travel to seek the knowledge of the Prophet ﷺ, as indeed travelling to seek knowledge is migration for the sake of Allah.'

Ṣafiyyah's parting advice to Imam Aḥmad رحمه الله exemplifies her absolute trust in Allah ﷻ. She did not have much to give to him for his journey, but she packed whatever she could and looked at him and said, 'O my son, indeed when Allah ﷻ is entrusted with something, He preserves it, and I am trusting you with Allah ﷻ, which is a trust that will never be lost.'

Imam Aḥmad رحمه الله went on to become one of the most influential scholars in the history of Islam. His mother's influence extended beyond her lifetime, with Imam Aḥmad attributing his success, piety, and accomplishments to her teachings. Her nurturing and guidance not only shaped his educational journey but also moulded his character and devotion to Allah ﷻ.

Imam Aḥmad's mother رحمها الله died when he was in his 30s. She was an example and role model for all mothers, with her life being a depiction of selfless devotion. Imam Aḥmad used to remember his mother and say, 'The most influential teacher I had was my mother. She taught me knowledge and she taught me how to live in this life with minimum need and ultimate focus on the Hereafter and Allah ﷻ.'

CHAPTER FIVE

Fāṭimah bint ʿAbbās al-Baghdādiyyah ﷺ

Bringing positive change to the lives of people is not an easy task. It takes courage, perseverance, and empathy. Some of the luminaries who reformed communities and changed lives were Muslim women who impacted their surroundings with their knowledge and wisdom. Among them was a prominent scholar and teacher by the name of Fāṭimah bint ʿAbbās al-Baghdādiyyah ﷺ.

A Scholar and Leader

Fāṭimah bint ʿAbbās al-Baghdādiyyah ﷺ, who was also known as Umm Zaynab, was a scholar, jurist, and leader of the women of her time. She was born and raised in Baghdad in the 7th century AH and was highly revered among her peers. Her dedication to knowledge, practice, and guiding others towards the path of righteousness is evident from the testimonies of prominent scholars like Ibn Taymiyyah and Imam al-Dhahabī ﷺ.

Shaykh al-Islām Ibn Taymiyyah ﷺ, who was the main teacher of Ibn al-Qayyim ﷺ, was one of the most prominent and renowned leaders and scholars of Islam. He was amazed by her knowledge and praised her intellect. Fāṭimah followed the Ḥanbalī school and knew al-Mughnī, the most famous book of the Ḥanbalī school of thought that consists of 15 volumes, completely by heart – a remarkable achievement that earned her recognition by prominent scholars, such as Shaykh Ibn Kathīr and Shaykh al-Dhahabī.

Commenting on her, Imam al-Dhahabī said, 'A sizeable number of women benefited from her and repented. She had an abundance of knowledge, was content with little, and keen to benefit people and give sermons with sincerity, God-consciousness, and for [the sake of] commanding the good.'

She moved from her birthplace of Baghdad to Damascus, and then to Cairo, where she influenced a lot of people. The women of Egypt were inspired by her and she was a highly respected figure in the community. She played a significant role in teaching the Qur'an to women and influencing generations of scholars, thereby highlighting her dedication to spreading knowledge.

Shaping a Virtuous Community

Besides her scholarly prowess, Fāṭimah was known for her character, humility, and piety. Imam al-Dhahabī praised her by describing her exceptional character and personality and said, 'I visited her and I adored her character, humility, and God-wariness. She knew fiqh well and Ibn Taymiyyah was amazed by her knowledge and intelligence.' She was a woman of great insight and was recognised for her wisdom and asceticism. She also played a pivotal role as a reformer and preacher, helping women reconnect with their faith during a critical period in Islamic history. Her efforts in promoting good and forbidding evil are a testament to her commitment to shaping a virtuous community.

In his famous book al-Bidāyah wa al-Nihāyah, Ibn Kathīr says, 'I heard Shaykh Taqī al-Dīn Ibn Taymiyyah praising her a lot and lauding her virtue and knowledge. He stated that she knew most of al-Mughnī, and he used to prepare himself for her juristic issues and questions due to her sharp understanding.'

Mentoring the Households of Scholars

Fāṭimah's influence was not confined to her own understanding of Islam. She taught a significant number of women, including the mother-in-law of Imam Ibn Kathīr. She was also the teacher of ʿĀ'ishah bint al-Ṣiddīq, the wife of Shaykh Jamāl al-Dīn al-Mizzī, a renowned Shāfiʿī scholar. ʿĀ'ishah bint al-Ṣiddīq in turn taught the wife of Imam Ibn Kathīr, Amah al-Raḥīm Zaynab.

Fāṭimah's legacy continues through the generations she influenced and the impact she made on the communities she lived in. Her reformative efforts and commitment to knowledge remain an inspiration for Muslims striving to better themselves and their societies. She lived in the time of Ibn Taymiyyah, and just as he is celebrated for his contributions, Fāṭimah bint ʿAbbās al-Baghdādiyyah's significance is equally noteworthy.

She died above the age of 80 in Cairo, Egypt, on the Day of ʿArafah in the month of Dhū al-Ḥijjah. Her passing was marked by a large funeral gathering, indicating the respect and admiration she garnered during her lifetime. Her resting place in al-Qarāfah is a reminder of her enduring impact.

Fāṭimah bint ʿAbbās al-Baghdādiyyah's story serves as a remarkable example of a woman who excelled as a scholar, teacher, reformer, and spiritual leader. Her contributions and influence reached far and wide, leaving a lasting impact on Islamic scholarship and the lives of countless individuals.

CHAPTER SIX

Fāṭimah al-Baṭayaḥiyyah ﵏

The role of women in learning and disseminating knowledge has always been imperative to the betterment of society. Some women dedicated their lives to righteous knowledge. They were mentors and teachers to great personalities who went on to become pioneers themselves. One character that assumes great space in this category is Fāṭimah al-Baṭayaḥiyyah ﵏. Born in the 8th century, a time when the Islamic civilisation was flourishing, she emerged as a luminary of knowledge and a scholar of great repute in the Hadith sciences. Her story is one of intellectual excellence and devotion to the pursuit of Islamic scholarship.

A Mentor to Eminent scholars

Fāṭimah bint Ibrāhīm ibn Maḥmūd al-Baṭayaḥiyyah ﵏ lived in Damascus, where she would spend her time teaching Hadith to students and was one of the greatest scholars of her period. There are no historical accounts or detailed narratives about her life, but her reputation rested firmly on the foundations of her knowledge and character, which became a projection of her qualities.

She was a mentor to many well-known scholars, and one of her most illustrious students was al-Bukhārī ﵀, a towering figure in Islamic scholarship whose collection of Hadith remains one of the most trusted and revered sources of Islamic law and practice. Besides al-Bukhārī, there were also many other male scholars who would come from all over the Muslim world to learn from her and meet her in person.

From the Blessed Land of the Prophet ﷺ

In the latter part of her life, Fāṭimah al-Baṭayaḥiyyah moved to Medina and taught her students in the mosque of the Prophet Muhammad ﷺ. She would teach in the vicinity of the Prophet's grave, and when fatigue overcame her, she would rest her head on the blessed grave and continue teaching.

While historical records offer only glimpses of Fāṭimah al-Baṭayaḥiyyah's life, her story serves as a poignant reminder of the pivotal role that women have played in the preservation and transmission of Islamic knowledge.

CHAPTER SEVEN

Fāṭimah al-Fihriyyah

Some change-makers bring a revolution with their actions and ideas, creating waves of growth and development for centuries abound. Fāṭimah al-Fihriyyah ☙ was one such woman, a remarkable pioneer in education who created a ground-breaking institution.

Building a Landmark

Fāṭimah al-Fihriyyah ☙ was born in the 9th century (800 CE) in Kairouan, Tunisia. Her father, Muhammad ibn ʿAbdullāh, was a merchant, and she grew up in a privileged home. When she was small, her father decided to relocate to Morocco with her and her sister. We do not know much about her personal life other than the fact that she was renowned for being a deep thinker. Her legacy, however, can be found in the memorable work she did and the landmark she built. Fāṭimah al-Fihriyyah ☙ was the founder of the University of al-Qarawiyyin in Fez, Morocco. The Qarawiyyin Mosque and college complex is renowned for being one of the oldest universities in the world.

How did a woman centuries ago establish an educational institute that is still running and thriving today? How did she get the resources and vision for something so magnificent? Fāṭimah al-Fihriyyah was a pious young woman who was extremely passionate about learning and imparting knowledge, and it was this passion that formed her vision.

Since she belonged to a prestigious family, her father's early death left her with a large inheritance. With her vision set on reforming education for others, she used this money to build a mosque and university where people could get authentic knowledge. The University and Mosque of al-Qarawiyyin was thus founded, named after her place of birth in Tunisia, al-Kairouan. It became the first and largest mosque and university complex in North Africa, educating students from all over the world. It is recognised by the United Nations Educational, Scientific and Cultural Organization (UNESCO) and the Guinness Book of Records as the first degree-granting university in the world. The al-Qarawiyyin Mosque and University was not merely a religious institution but also a centre of learning that embraced various disciplines, including Islamic studies, astronomy, philosophy, and more.

Amongst the alumni of the university are some of the most prominent Muslim scholars, including Ibn Khaldūn, a famous philosopher, as well as the jurist and thinker Ibn Rushd. The university was also attended by Christians like Pope Sylvester II, who introduced Arabic numerals to Europe. The fact that al-Qarawiyyin University produced scholars who influenced not only the Muslim world but also Europe and beyond speaks to the transformative power of education across borders and cultures. Al-Qarawiyyin University precedes the University of Bologna by approximately 100 years, and the mosque is one of the most ancient in the world, dating back even further than the mosque in

Timbuktu. The historically rich and impressive library of al-Qarawiyyin University is one of the oldest in the world, containing more than 4,000 manuscripts.

A Pioneer and Seeker of Knowledge

Fāṭimah al-Fihriyyah's thirst for knowledge and learning was unbound, and when she was 59, she enrolled herself in the university and graduated. Despite being the founder of such a prestigious educational institute and becoming a role model for many, she continued on her own path of knowledge. Her diploma was written on a piece of wood and is still kept safe in the university.

Fāṭimah's story serves as a reminder that women have played pivotal roles in shaping history. The Qarawiyyin University's enduring presence and its continuous commitment to education stand as a living tribute to Fāṭimah al-Fihriyyah's vision and legacy. Her impact has extended far beyond her time, influencing scholars, researchers, and students for centuries. Her determination, foresight, and courage broke down barriers and opened doors for future generations, thus showcasing that women can be leaders, innovators, and change-makers with the help of Allah ﷻ.

CHAPTER EIGHT

Fāṭimah bint Muhammad ibn Aḥmad al-Samarqandiyyah ﵩ

The prevailing notion that Islam subjugates women is a misconception rooted in the way we practise the faith today. Many people hold to the idea that women in the Islamic and post-Islamic eras took a backseat when it came to education or other noteworthy intellectual achievements. However, this could not be further from the truth, as we find accounts of numerous Muslim women who were torchbearers and pioneers in educational and religious scholarship. A name that stands out among these is Fāṭimah al-Samarqandiyyah ﵩ, an extraordinary woman of flawless character who possessed a wealth of knowledge and a legacy with her countless contributions to Islamic history.

An Emerging Scholar and Jurist

Fāṭimah al-Samarqandiyyah ﵩ was the daughter of a great scholar of Islam, Muhammed ibn Aḥmad al-Samarqandī ﵀. He was a prominent jurist and author of Tuḥfah al-Fuqahā', a famous book in the Ḥanafī school of thought. He passed away in 539 AH (1144 CE) and was known for his righteousness and for devoting his entire life to seeking and conveying knowledge to his students and family.

Fāṭimah al-Samarqandiyyah's exact date of birth is unknown, but it is recorded that she was born in the 12th century in Samarkand, the third-largest city in present-day Uzbekistan and one of the oldest inhabited cities in Central Asia. When she was born, the city was under the control of the Mongols, and the populace was largely oppressed. She was not from the time of the Prophet ﷺ, nor did she see the Companions or the Caliphs, but under her father's guidance, Fāṭimah ؓ blossomed into a scholar of unparalleled depth and wisdom.

Her education transcended the boundaries of ritualistic worship, encompassing the intricacies of fasting, almsgiving, ʿUmrah and Hajj, business transactions, inheritance laws, marriage, and the principles of enjoining good and preventing evil. She directly learned from her father, who was her greatest teacher and mentor, and became a specialist in Islamic jurisprudence, Quranic sciences, and Hadith to the extent that she was granted the authority to issue rulings on various matters. Her rulings were written in her handwriting and also included her father's signature.

A Consultant for Knowledge

When Fāṭimah ؓ reached a marriageable age, it was reported that she received proposals from many rich and powerful men who could offer her the luxuries of the world. However, her father had a different vision for her. ʿAlā' al-Dīn Abū Bakr ibn Masʿūd al-Kāsānī ؒ was a student of Fāṭimah's father. The former wrote a commentary on Tuḥfah al-Fuqahā' called Badā'i' al-Ṣanā'i', an eight-volume work that later became a classic. He was a great scholar himself, and Fāṭimah's father was so impressed with his work that he gave his daughter's hand to him in marriage. Their union was a unique one, as al-Kāsānī's book became the dowry (mahr) for her marriage with him.

After their marriage, the scholarly couple lived in the same house as Fāṭimah's father, which resulted in the formation of an informal fiqh committee that would find solutions to problems related to jurisprudence. Despite his considerable knowledge, al-Kāsānī often turned to Fāṭimah when he faced complex fiqh questions. Her wisdom and guidance became invaluable, and she would put her signature alongside his on critical matters – a testament to her exceptional grasp of Islamic jurisprudence.

Ibn al-'Adīm, the famous 13th century biographer of Aleppo, said: 'My father narrated that "her husband sometimes had doubts and erred in the issuing of a fatwa. She would then tell him the correct opinion and explain the reason for his mistake".' The students of Fāṭimah's husband narrated that whenever her husband would receive a hard fiqh question, he would go home and get back with a detailed answer to the question. This happened often, so they understood that al-Kāsānī would go home and consult with Fāṭimah al-Samarqandiyyah whenever he could not solve a certain issue alone.

An Esteemed Advisor and Philanthropist

One of her lesser-known qualities was her calligraphic skills. Her beautiful and intricate writing would create the rulings, creating pieces of art that were highly respected and reliable.

Fāṭimah's influence extended far beyond her home. She and her husband made a courageous decision to move to Syria, a land brimming with Islamic knowledge. She was shown great courtesy there, and her wisdom and scholarship attracted the attention of the notable figures of her time, including Nūr al-Dīn Zengī ﵀, the mentor of the great Ṣalāḥ al-Dīn al-Ayyūbī ﵀. Fāṭimah became his trusted advisor and personal counsellor in matters of religion and fiqh. It was a journey of sacrifice, both in physical and mental terms. Leaving behind the comforts of her home and establishing a life in a new place mirrored her internal journey towards a great pursuit of knowledge.

Fāṭimah's piety and compassion were equally remarkable. She was not just a jurist and scholar but also an exceptionally charitable person who put the needs of others before hers. In Aleppo, during the sacred month of Ramadan, Fāṭimah ﵀ exhibited an extraordinary act of charity. She sold her own bracelets to provide meals for scholars and students, an act that would go on to inspire generations. She was, in fact, the pioneer of the noble tradition of providing ifṭār for those who were fasting.

Fāṭimah al-Samarqandiyyah's journey through life was one of unceasing dedication to both knowledge and piety. She passed away in Aleppo in about 1185 CE, leaving behind a legacy that continues to inspire and benefit Islamic scholarship. Her husband lived after her for about six years. Her story is a testament to the power of women in Islam, a reminder that their contributions to knowledge and faith have shaped the course of history and continue to guide us today. She dedicated herself to the lifelong pursuit of righteous knowledge and illuminated the path of many others on the way.

CHAPTER NINE

Fāṭimah bint Ḥamad al-Fuḍayliyyah

One of the characteristics of a noble person is that they exhibit the qualities they are teaching through their actions and behaviour. Their dealings with people and reactions to various situations reflect their beliefs, and they adopt an approach of kindness, humility, and gratitude at every stage of life. One such personality was Fāṭimah bint Ḥamad al-Fuḍayliyyah, a woman whose legacy resonates with profound significance and whose remarkable contributions to Islamic history are admirable.

A Distinguished Title

Fāṭimah bint Ḥamad al-Fuḍayliyyah was also known as al-Shaykhah al-Fuḍayliyyah – a title given to her by prominent scholars of her time. In the 18th and 19th century, a period witnessing intellectual novelties, Fāṭimah al-Fuḍayliyyah emerged as a formidable figure of knowledge. She was a Hadith scholar (muḥaddithah), jurist (faqīhah), and was considered one of the last scholars in a long line of Hadith figures. Her dedication to the study of Hadith and jurisprudence earned her a distinguished place among the eminent muḥaddithāt (female Hadith scholars) of her era. She held fast to the chain of narration, ensuring that the knowledge of Hadith continued to flow through her as she stood as one of its last guardians. Shaykh Akram Nadwi mentioned her contributions in his book about the muḥaddithāt and praised her prowess, which extended into various spheres of Islamic knowledge, including principles of fiqh, jurisprudence, and Quranic exegesis.

Based in the sacred city of Mecca, she inspired and guided both men and women in their journey to attain Islamic knowledge. Her scholarly lectures were attended by eminent male Hadith scholars, which included ʿUmar al-Ḥanafī and Muhammad Ṣāliḥ, who studied with her, received certificates from her, and acknowledged her expertise.

Leading by Example

The life of Fāṭimah al-Fuḍayliyyah was marked by the virtues of piety, righteousness, and asceticism. She personified the ideal of aligning knowledge with practice, a lesson relevant for seekers of knowledge across the ages. As the carriers of the Qur'an, it is our moral imperative to act upon the values and principles we impart to others and become role models for them. Those who learn and treasure the Qur'an and understand the huge responsibility it brings with it cannot be careless about its teachings. They must be distinguished in their actions, behaviour, and dealings to set an example for those around them. These were the principles that Fāṭimah al-Fuḍayliyyah lived by. She embodied the essence of complete detachment from worldly possessions and became a guiding light for many.

An interesting fact about her that illustrates her deep love for writing was her calligraphy. She excelled in this art, receiving diplomas from many scholars and was highly regarded for writing books in calligraphy.

A Treasure of Knowledge

Before she passed away in 1831, Fāṭimah al-Fuḍayliyyah founded a public library in Mecca, where she settled towards the end of her life. This library became a beacon of light, brimming with the treasure of knowledge and keeping her memory alive for generations to come. Shaykhah Fāṭimah al-Fuḍayliyyah was a role model for women. She was an expert in the Islamic sciences but, most importantly, she was a woman who exhibited the golden principles she taught to others. Her words were in complete harmony with her actions. She lived a life of simplicity and left a mark in our history with her admirable character, righteousness, and deep wisdom.

ʿĀʾISHAH BINT AL-SHĀṬIʾ ﷠

* ◆ ◆ ◆ *

Her published work spans over a period of 60 years and made her the most accomplished female scholar of the 20th century.

CHAPTER TEN

ʿĀʾishah Muhammad ʿAlī ʿAbd al-Raḥmān ﷺ

Seeking knowledge and teaching have always been passions for women in Islamic history, with many of them often leaving their mark within the realm of education. One such impressionable woman was ʿĀʾishah Muhammad bint ʿAbd al-Raḥmān ﷺ, a legendary student, teacher, and researcher. Her journey from a small city in Egypt to becoming one of the most accomplished female scholars of the 20th century is truly inspiring.

An Academic Legacy

Born in 1912 in Dimyat, a small city in Egypt on the Mediterranean shores, ʿĀʾishah ﷺ completed primary schooling at home. She is known widely by her nickname, Bint al-Shāṭiʾ (lit. The Daughter of the Shore), because she was born close to the coastline. ʿĀʾishah bint al-Shāṭiʾʾs dedication to learning and education is evident in her pursuit of knowledge, as she went on to study Arabic and attained a doctorate in the Arabic language. Her ambition was to pursue an academic career, and she ended up becoming a professor at two of the most prestigious universities in the Arab world: Ain Shams University in Cairo, and al-Qarawiyyin University in Fez. In the latter, she presided as a professor of tafsīr of the Qur'an.

One of the most significant events in her life that contributed to her professional and personal growth was her marriage with Amīn Khūlī, who was a prominent Muslim scholar. He was a great inspiration in her life and helped her immensely in her academic and intellectual journey. 'Ā'ishah bint al-Shāṭi' was deeply grateful to him for his guidance, and this is possibly the reason for why she dedicated all her writings to him, whether they were in the form of books or research papers. Her husband described her as the disciple of the literary school that he belonged to and the lady of the house that he resided in.

Leaving a Mark on the World

'Ā'ishah bint al-Shāṭi''s legacy is particularly marked by her contributions to Islamic studies and Arabic literature. She taught as a professor for more than 50 years, teaching and guiding students from all over the world, especially from Lebanon, Egypt, Sudan, and the North African region. Her most unique and extraordinary work is the commentary on the last 14 sūrahs of the Qur'an called al-Tafsīr al-Bayānī, which is a testament to her dedication and scholarly genius. It took her eight years to write, and is undoubtedly one of her most famous theological texts. Despite the societal norms of her time, where education for women was a non-existent concept, she not only became a highly intellectual professor but also had a deep impact on many people around her.

She gave special emphasis to combining Islamic studies and the Arabic language and always referred to both interchangeably, believing that religious and linguistic knowledge are not mutually exclusive but mutually enriching.

Honoured for Her Values

ʿĀ'ishah bint al-Shāṭi' was committed to empowering women and advocating for their rights, while adhering to the values of Islam. She was an example of a strong and educated woman contributing to society through her remarkable achievements. She was not deterred by the lack of resources in her time but made use of every opportunity.

Her influence extended beyond her teaching and writing, as she left an indelible mark on her students and on the wider Muslim community. ʿĀ'ishah bint al-Shāṭi' left behind a legacy of extraordinary literary works in the form of more than 40 books on the Islamic fields, dozens of books on Arabic literature, novels, hundreds of research papers, and innumerable articles in daily and weekly newspapers. Her published work spans over a period of 60 years and made her the most accomplished female scholar of the 20th century. The government of Egypt recognised and honoured her after her death by issuing commemorative stamps bearing her liking.

ʿĀ'ishah bint al-Shāṭi' passed away in 1998 at the age of 85, having lived a memorable and impactful life. Her legacy continues to inspire generations of Muslim women to pursue knowledge, engage in intellectual discourse, and empower themselves with the teachings of the Qur'an.

CHAPTER ELEVEN

Fāṭimah bint ʿAbd al-Malik

People with influence and power generally develop a sense of pride and arrogance, but Islam teaches us to turn these privileges into opportunities for goodness. Some women in Muslim history had such power and status as they belonged to noble families, but they developed a personality of humility and God-consciousness and led lives of simplicity. Fāṭimah bint ʿAbd al-Malik was one such woman. Born into an abundance of riches, she gave it all up for a simple life of piety and modesty.

Born into Nobility and Luxury

Fāṭimah bint ʿAbd al-Malik was born in a prestigious household. She belonged to the Banū Umayyah and was a princess by lineage, as she was the daughter of the Caliph ʿAbd al-Malik ibn Marwān ibn al-Ḥakam, the leader of the Muslims at the time of Umayyad rule in Damascus. The Banū Umayyah governed immediately after Sayyidunā ʿAlī was killed and took over to assume rule over the Muslim world. Fāṭimah was raised in a home of nobility and leadership, and due to this early exposure to an environment of luxury and power, she was familiar with royal culture and conducted herself with dignity and grace.

Her father devoted a lot of love and care into raising his beloved daughter, paying special attention to her education and intellectual development. This early investment in her education later proved pivotal in shaping the course of her life. She learnt from eminent scholars of her time and her education spanned a broad spectrum of subjects, including poetry, Quranic studies, Islamic legislation, and history. Despite being the favourite of her father and living a life of privileges, she neither developed a sense of entitlement nor became arrogant; instead, she grew up to be a woman of beautiful character and morality.

After her paternal uncle and the governor of Egypt, ʿAbd al-ʿAzīz ibn Marwān, passed away, her father brought his son, ʿUmar ibn ʿAbd al-ʿAzīz رحمه الله, to Damascus, where he was raised. He was the great-grandson of Sayyidunā ʿUmar ibn al-Khaṭṭāb رضي الله عنه, as his mother was Sayyidunā ʿUmar's granddaughter. When she became of marriageable age, Fāṭimah's father married her to her cousin, ʿUmar ibn ʿAbd al-ʿAzīz رحمه الله, and sent him to Medina as a governor. Fāṭimah continued to live a life of luxury in Medina until an unfortunate event happened. ʿUmar ibn ʿAbd al-ʿAzīz was stripped of his position as the governor due to his refusal to welcome al-Ḥajjāj ibn Yūsuf in Medina, who was the governor of Baghdad and an extremely unjust ruler.

Choosing a Life of Simplicity

This event prompted the couple to move back to Damascus. Tragically, Fāṭimah's father passed away during this period, and 'Umar ibn 'Abd al-'Azīz ﷺ ascended to the position of the Caliph, the leader of the Muslim ummah. He was called the Fifth Caliph of Islam after the Four Rightly Guided Caliphs due to his just and devout leadership, and was one of the finest rulers in Muslim history. It is said that at the time of 'Umar ibn 'Abd al-'Azīz, there were no poor people in the Muslim ummah to give zakat to. It is reported that he had many of the characteristics and qualities of Sayyidunā 'Umar ibn al-Khaṭṭāb ﷺ. When Fāṭimah ﷺ was faced with a choice of either living a humble life with her husband or choosing a comfortable life of luxuries with her family, she chose the former. She lived a life of asceticism with her husband and donated all her possessions to the treasury of the Muslim state.

Their life in Damascus was challenging, marked by a scarcity in the most basic of necessities. There were nights when they lacked blankets to shield themselves from the harsh winter cold. Fāṭimah used to say, 'How I wish that the distance between us and the caliphate was as large as the distance between the East and the West! For by Allah ﷻ, we have not seen happiness since the caliphate has been brought to us.' She was a woman of modesty and piety and longed for a simple life away from power and grandeur.

Fāṭimah bint 'Abd al-Malik's legacy was one of selflessness and service. It was narrated that one day a woman came from Iraq to get approval for the allowance for her orphan daughters. She saw the first lady baking bread by herself and sat near her. She was looking at the condition of the house and after seeing its poor state, she said regretfully that she had come to find some favours from that house, but the house itself looked like it was in need. Fāṭimah ﵍, the wife of the Caliph said, 'Your homes are cared for at the cost of ours.' She inquired about the woman's problems and put her case before the Caliph, who approved the allowance for them.

An Embodiment of Beautiful Character

Fāṭimah bint ʿAbd al-Malik ﵍ was a woman who was born with wealth and was bred with royal manners, but she withdrew from that life to stand by her husband and live in service of others. She was not a scholar, nor did she possess many academic accolades and titles, yet her most notable quality was that she was a woman of action and practical application. She embodied the teachings of Islam by becoming a source of goodness to society. She lived long after her husband died, but persisted in her simple lifestyle. Later in her life, she married Dāwūd ibn Sulaymān ibn Marwān.

The noted Turkish writer, Dhehni Afindi, writes: 'Fāṭimah bint ʿAbd al-Malik was known as Dhāt al-Khimār, i.e. the Woman of the Shawl'. She was given this title due to her ḥayā' (modesty), signifying her embodiment of humility and simplicity. Her legacy was not one of traditional knowledge but a knowledge of practice and selfless service. Thus, Fāṭimah bint ʿAbd al-Malik's life stands as a testament to the enduring value of kindness and benevolence.

CHAPTER TWELVE

Salmā bint al-Jazarī

Knowledge and education are common themes in women who have left a mark in history. A special place among them is occupied by Muslim women, who delved into the study of the Qur'an and Hadith and left a treasure of knowledge behind them for the benefit of the coming generations.

A Journey of Knowledge and Love for Qur'an

Salmā bint al-Jazarī was the beloved daughter of Abū al-Khayr Muhammad ibn Muhammad Shams al-Dīn Ibn al-Jazarī. He was a great Imam in the field of qirā'āt, the various recitations of the Qur'an, and a distinguished scholar in Damascus. Born in Damascus on 25 Ramadan 751 AH to a prominent and righteous businessman, Imam al-Jazarī excelled in the sciences of the Qur'an and Hadith and travelled extensively to gain knowledge on these two subjects. He travelled through Damascus, Mecca, Medina, and Egypt to learn recitation styles from around 40 scholars. He instilled the same love for knowledge and the Quranic modes of recitation in his daughter, Salmā bint al-Jazarī, who also pursued her quest for knowledge and studied the readings of the Qur'an.

Salmā bint al-Jazarī embarked on her journey of the memorisation of the Qur'an at the age of 13. She soon memorised and mastered the book Introduction to Tajwīd (Muqaddimah al-Tajwīd), as well as the book Introduction to Arabic Grammar (Muqaddimah al-Naḥw). She was an excellent student and followed in the footsteps of her father, learning with sincerity and dedication. Her father praised her knowledge and recitation of the Qur'an in his book Ghāyah al-Nihāyah, and even called her The Mother of Good – Umm al-Khayr.

A Proficient Reciter

In addition to this, Salmā bint al-Jazarī also memorised the book Ṭayyibah al-Nashr fī al-Qirā'āt al-'Ashr, a poem written by her father on the ten Quranic readings. She mastered the ten modes of recitation and finished memorising the Qur'an on the 12th of Rabī' al-Awwal, specifically in the year 832 AH.

Salmā bint al-Jazarī was an excellent ḥāfiẓah and proficient reciter. Her recitations were unmatched. Besides her religious accolades, she also excelled in academics and mastered the Arabic and Persian languages. She was known to have beautiful handwriting and her intellectual expertise extended to the study of Hadith, where she reached a level of proficiency that enabled her to independently engage with the sacred texts. Through rigorous study and unwavering commitment, Salmā bint al-Jazarī emerged as a luminary in the realm of Quranic scholarship, etching her name in the books of history.

CHAPTER THIRTEEN

Maryam Jameelah ﷺ

We end the book with a story of faith in times of utter confusion. A story of a woman who chose Islam at a place and time when it was buried under layers of misapprehension and false claims. The story of Maryam Jameelah and her effortless search for faith, her whole-hearted acceptance of it, and the life she dedicated to embodying its teachings is remarkable.

Searching for the Truth

Maryam Jameelah ﷺ was a Muslim revert and Islamic scholar who – despite her secular upbringing and environment – found the light of Islam in her youth and did outstanding religious and intellectual work.

Jameelah ﷺ was born in New Rochelle, New York State, on 23 May 1934, and was named Margaret Marcus. As a fourth-generation American of German Jewish descent, her early years were spent being surrounded by American culture. She received a secular American education in the local public schools of Westchester, proving herself to be an exceptional student willing to learn and explore. From an early age, Maryam displayed a voracious appetite for knowledge. Libraries became her second home, where she delved into the subjects of religion, philosophy, history, anthropology, sociology, and biology.

Upon graduating from secondary school in 1952, she enrolled in New York University, where she studied a general liberal arts program. She developed a keen interest in religion at the age of nineteen while at university. However, her education was disrupted in 1953 due to severe illness, compelling her to temporarily withdraw from college without attaining a diploma. For two years, she grappled with her ailment, becoming confined to private and public hospitals. It was after she regained her health and was discharged from medical care that she found her passion and talent for writing.

Embracing Islam with Heart

Writing became Maryam's solace, such that she went on to pen several books and religious works in the future. Looking for spiritual guidance, she started searching and exploring different religions and ideologies, and it was during this examination that she found Islam in 1954. She was inspired by the work of Muhammad Asad, a Muslim scholar and intellect who reverted to Islam from Judaism. His autobiography The Road to Mecca and famous book Islam at the Crossroads were a big influence on her decision to become a Muslim.

In the presence of Shaykh Daoud Ahmad Faisal, she embraced Islam on 24 May 1961, at the Islamic Mission in Brooklyn, New York. It did not take long for her to change her name from Margaret Marcus to Maryam Jameelah. This marked the beginning of her journey to Islamic knowledge. She read and learnt extensively about this beautiful religion and became vocal about its message. She was a staunch advocate for the rights of the Palestinians and supported Muslim causes despite facing opposition from her family.

Soon after she reverted to Islam, Maryam started writing for a Muslim magazine in Durban, South Africa. The articles she wrote presented her views on the ideology of the true religion, Islam, and concerns about the Western portrayal of it. As such, she sought to debate the critics of Islam, all of whom sought to tarnish its image. It was through this journal that she became aware of the works of Mawlānā Sayyid Abu al-A'la Mawdudi, who also contributed to the journal and was the founder of the Jamat-e-Islami Party in Pakistan.

A New Life

Maryam Jameelah was inspired by Mawlānā Sayyid Abu al-A'la Mawdudi's writings and work, and they began corresponding through letters, discussing various issues and concerns about religion, as well as her personal spiritual dilemma. In 1962, Mawlānā Mawdudi extended an invitation for her to relocate to Pakistan and become an integral part of his family in Lahore. She accepted this offer, and a year later, she became the second wife of Muhammad Yusuf Khan, a dedicated worker for Jamat-e-Islami, who later became the publisher of her literary legacy.

In the years that followed, Maryam became the mother of five children, with the first dying in infancy. She continued to live in a large extended family with her co-wife and in-laws. Remarkably, she maintained her intellectual pursuits and literary endeavours even after marriage, exemplifying a balance rarely seen in married women. In fact, her most important pieces of writing were done during and in between her pregnancies.

Maryam harboured a profound aversion to atheism and materialism in all their various forms. Her quest for transcendent ideals led her to champion Islam as the most profound explanation of the ultimate truth. Her ceaseless discussions and debates on critical Islamic issues, as well as her unapologetic critique of Western ideologies, positioned her as a prominent figure within Muslim societies. She ardently opposed orientalism, leaving an indelible mark on the Muslim youth through her writings.

An Advocate for Islamic Revival

Maryam Jameelah was an advocate for the rejuvenation of Islamic thought with unwavering conviction. She was also extremely concerned with the disparity of religion and Islam in the West and how the immoral ideologies were corrupting societies. Her extensive body of work includes notable titles such as Islam Versus the West, Islam and Modernism, Islam in Theory and Practice, Islam Versus Ahl al-Kitab: Past and Present, The Generation Gap: Its Cause and Consequences, Islam and Orientalism, Islam and Modern Men, and Ahmad Khalil: The Story of a Palestinian Arab Refugee and His Family. In the course of her life, Maryam wrote around 30 books on Islamic values and culture that continue to enlighten and motivate both youth and adults alike.

On 31 October 2012, after facing a prolonged battle with illness, Maryam Jameelah departed from this world in Lahore, leaving behind a legacy of scholarly interest, unyielding faith, and profound intellectual contributions to Islam.

Notes

Notes

Notes